THE DESERT PRINCE

Paul B. Ricchiuti

TEACH Services, Inc.
PUBLISHING
www.TEACHServices.com • (800) 367-1844

World rights reserved. This book or any portion thereof may not be copied or reproduced in any form or manner whatever, except as provided by law, without the written permission of the publisher, except by a reviewer who may quote brief passages in a review.

The author assumes full responsibility for the accuracy of all facts and quotations as cited in this book. The opinions expressed in this book are the author's personal views and interpretations, and do not necessarily reflect those of the publisher.

This book is provided with the understanding that the publisher is not engaged in giving spiritual, legal, medical, or other professional advice. If authoritative advice is needed, the reader should seek the counsel of a competent professional.

Copyright © 2021 Paul B. Ricchiuti
Copyright © 2021 TEACH Services, Inc.
ISBN-13: 978-1-4796-1260-4 (Paperback)
ISBN-13: 978-1-4796-1261-1 (ePub)
Library of Congress Control Number: 2021941097

All Scripture quotations, unless otherwise indicated, are taken from the King James Version® of the Bible. Public domain.

Scripture quotations marked RSV are taken from the Revised Standard Version of the Bible, copyright © 1946, 1952, and 1971 the Division of Christian Education of the National Council of the Churches of Christ in the United States of America. Used by permission. All rights reserved.

Scripture quotations marked MEV are taken from the Modern English Version. Copyright © 2014 by Military Bible Association. Used by permission. All rights reserved.

Scripture quotations marked NKJV are taken from the New King James Version®. Copyright © 1990 by Thomas Nelson. Used by permission. All rights reserved.

Scripture quotations marked TLB are taken from The Living Bible, Copyright © 1971 by Tyndale House Foundation. Used by permission.

Published by

www.TEACHServices.com • (800) 367-1844

Dedication

As Joshua was to Moses,
so is this book dedicated to
my adoptive son, Paul Jansen.

Author's Disclaimer

The author has made every attempt to verify all facts and circumstances presented in this story. However, given the lack of available detailed information, he has taken the liberty of portraying certain events in the light of how he believes they most likely occurred.

Contents

Introduction . . . . *vii*

1. A Small Basket 9
2. The Key 14
3. He Ran 20
4. Teachers on Four Legs 25
5. Those Forty Long Years 30
6. It Didn't Burn 34
7. He Went 39
8. God's Amazing Weapons 46
9. A Strange Dinner 51
10. Go 55
11. Night the Angel Came 59
12. They Sang and Danced 67
13. Shur 70
14. Up in the Air 77
15. Would They Say YES? 82

16. Forty Days 85

17. Weeds and a Veil 92

18. Strange Fire. 98

19. Meat. 102

20. Kadesh 106

21. Korah 111

22. Ten Times Four-XL 120

23. So Close. 126

24. Giants 131

25. The Donkey Asked Why. 135

26. It Is Time 140

Afterword *144*

Bibliography *148*

Introduction

Although Moses lived thousands of years ago, he is alive today. Proof for this comes from the Bible. Matthew 17 has the story. The setting is on a mountainside.

We read, "Jesus took Peter, James, and John his brother, led them up on a high mountain by themselves; and He was transfigured before them. [Transfigure: the supernatural and glorified change in the appearance of Jesus on the mountain, also, a change in outward form or appearance. From *Webster New Explorer Dictionary, 3rd edition*.] His face shone like the sun, and His clothes became as white as the light. And behold, **Moses** and Elijah appeared to them, talking with Him" (Matt. 17:1–3, NKJV, emphasis added).

Moses had died long before this happened, but Elijah never died, yet there they were, all three of them alive and together. These two men came to see Jesus for one reason, and one reason only. It was to assure Him of His Father's love and that His approval was with Him through the ordeal He was about to suffer. Jesus needed this from His Father for as horrible as it was to be. He also knew the entire universe would be watching the unbelievable display of God's love for a fallen race. Enormous pressure lay heavy on Jesus.

From her book *The Desire of Ages*, Ellen White wrote, "**Moses** upon the mount of transfiguration was a witness to Christ's victory over sin and death. He represented those who shall come forth from the grave at the resurrection of the just" (pp. 421, 422, emphasis added).

She also wrote, "Moses passed under the dominion of death, but he was not to remain in the tomb. Christ Himself called him forth to life" (*The Desire of Ages*, p. 421).

Did Jesus have the right to bring Moses back to life? YES, He did!

It was because "On the cross of Calvary He [Jesus] paid the redemption price [His life] of the race. And thus He gained the right to take the captives from the grasp of the great deceiver [Lucifer (Satan)]" (*The SDA Bible Commentary*, vol. 7, p. 952).

When Moses died, Satan tried to claim his body. Jesus waved him aside with these words, "The Lord rebuke [repulse or drive away sharply] you" (Jude 9, RSV). Thus, as Moses was raised to life, Satan knew he had been defeated. *He lost!*

The life and times of Moses are well known especially among Christians. People across the globe have repeated the story of this man countless times, and it is hard to understand the how and why a prince, under the Pharaoh of Egypt, decided to turn his back on wealth and power to lead a nation of slaves and rebels to a better life. But that is exactly what he did through God.

This introduction is only one story of the countless others whose eyes looked for and found a happy, more meaningful future.

Many are the actors on the stage of good and evil. History records their stories. It also describes the actors—good and evil alike. However, the obedience and loyalty of those who follow God overrides hate, treason, lust, and greed that others may choose.

This is the true story of one man who faced the odds and won. Even with his faults, he came off more than conqueror. The man Moses.

Paul B. Ricchiuti

1

A Small Basket

The River Nile is about 4,160 miles long. In places it can be quite wide. Two other rivers compete for being the longest water systems on earth. These are the Yangtze in China and the Amazon in South America. The Nile, however, is in the lead. It has various names, the el Bahr, the en-Nil, and the el-Bahr en-Nil. It is composed of three powerful streams, the White Nile, the Blue Nile, and the Atbara. All come together, however, as one river when they reach the Mediterranean Sea. The White Nile is the largest and fullest, the Blue Nile is the longest. The Blue Nile and the Atbara are the muddiest.

Rising in the highlands of eastern Africa, these three streams run swiftly north through seemingly endless miles of dry desert wasteland that burn with scorching sand and heat until it finally reaches the city of Cairo and the Mediterranean Sea. This river is a symbol of life for thousands who make their home along its fertile banks. Is it any wonder then why ancient pyramid builders considered it sacred? They drank its water, bathed in it, watered herds and flocks and flooded fields to grow crops. It became a god, one they could see, feel, and use. It was the only thing flowing through the center of their vast empire that gave them the one ingredient valued most: life. This, however, became second only to the great Pharaoh himself, whom they considered the supreme object of worship.

One day, floating on those sacred waters, there bounced a small basket lined with pitch. Thus, our story begins. Hatshepsut, daughter of Pharaoh Thutmose I, went to the river to bathe. While doing so, she heard what sounded like a baby's cry. Curiosity took over. The princess ordered one of her attendants to wade through the water, following the sound. It led to a covered basket, and the sound she heard was coming from inside. It grew stronger. Carefully lifting the lid, she was shocked to find a tiny baby. It was a boy and he was unhappy (Exod. 2:3–6).

Motherly instinct took over as she reached out and held the child in her arms. Instantly she praised the river god for giving her this gift, the longing desire to have a son. She had no children of her own, but now, thanks to the god of the river, that had changed.

In a book titled *Genealogical Chronology of the World Before Christ* by Albert Wells, I read this passage: "Having rescued the child, its extreme beauty induced her to take it home and rear it as her own" (p. 110).

Through this passage we learn more about the pagan beliefs of these ancient people, for as mentioned, the Nile was considered sacred. It not only promised long life, but great prosperity as well. Therefore, these people assumed the river had to be a god, or a gift from one. There were many benefits, and this god could be seen. Its benefits turned dry sand into green fields that produced food. Trees and bushes gave fruit in abundance. The entire empire, peasants and royalty alike, bowed before these so-called deities in awe. Millions of Egyptians knew nothing about the one true God, the Creator of heaven and earth. Most were uneducated in higher learning, yet gifted in art, the building trade, politics, and warfare. At the same time their slaves, living in Goshen, knew and worshiped just one God; the only true God. But Egyptians considered those people as work animals. Their function was to obey, work, and serve them.

Given time, however, these two schools of thought were destined to clash, and clash they did because of a basket, a baby, and a royal princess.

Leviticus 26:12 states this about God's people, "And I will walk among you, and will be your God, and ye shall be my people."

Now, what about that small basket on the river with a baby inside? The Bible tells us that Miriam, a slave girl and sister of the baby, had been watching and following the basket. When she saw the princess claim the baby as her own, she bravely walked up to Pharaoh's daughter asking, "Shall I go and call to thee a nurse of the Hebrew women, that she may nurse the child for thee? [The answer was] ... Go. [Meaning yes] And the maid went and called the child's mother" (Exod. 2:7, 8). God's hand was in all this. He had plans for that child.

Let's pause for an ongoing question as to who the real mother of the baby was. There are several schools of thought on this; however, the Bible is clear, the mother was a Hebrew, but the boy needed training and skill to fill God's plans for leading a nation of slaves to freedom. The court and power of Pharaoh could do this.

Family intrigue surrounded Hatshepsut's (the princess') life. She knew that Moses was one of many in the royal household and that other children of Pharaoh wanted control of the throne. Because of this, Hatshepsut closely protected Moses.

A reasonable deduction from biblical chronology based on 1 Kings 6:1, and other supporting statements such as *The Great Controversy*, page 399, is that the Exodus took place about the middle of the fifteenth century BC. This date leads one to the conclusion that Moses grew up under Thutmose I [1525–1508 BC] and Queen Hatshepsut [the supposed aunt of Moses in 1504–1582 BC].

Hatshepsut was a remarkable woman. She had been the only legitimate child of Thutmose I and was married to her half-brother Thutmose II in order that he might legitimately succeed his father upon the throne. But the legitimate marriage of Thutmose II, like that of his father, again failed to provide a male heir. When Thutmose II died, after a reign of only four years, the priests of Amen, in a sudden coup, crowned an illegitimate son of Thutmose II, who was at that time a mere boy and served in the temple as a minor priest. In as much as Thutmose III, as he was later known, was too young to reign, his aunt Hatshepsut acted as regent for twenty-two years. Her reign was a peaceful one. She built great temples and erected huge obelisks. Supported by a powerful prime minister, Senenmut, Hatshepsut occupied the throne for twenty-two years; then she and Senenmut disappear from the record. Succeeding her, Thutmose III erased her name from all monuments in an attempt to eradicate the memory of her from the history of Egypt. This fact lends weight to the supposition that he removed her from the throne, and that she and Senenmut died violent deaths.

"When Moses was born, Hatshepsut was merely the daughter of Thutmose I. Moses's birth occurred many years before her marriage to her half-brother Thutmose II, and more than 20 years before she began her personal reign, after the death of her husband" (*SDA Bible Commentary*, Vol. 1, p. 502).

A question comes up. How is it that a slave girl could walk up freely to royalty and not only feel free to talk with one of them but also make a suggestion? Could it be that she was known in the palace? Royalty had many slaves doing their work, both young and old. Was she one of them? Notice the text. It called Miriam a maid, not a maiden. Is this a clue?

Here is a suggestion. Could it be her age, or that the palace and its vast complex, was constantly surrounded by swarms of servants, including children? If this was the case, a small slave girl's appearance, especially if she were seen often, was common and not unusual. She apparently posed no threat. The accepted theory is that angels were in constant control of the entire situation.

Author Wells had another somewhat unusual insight as to why the princess decided to have a Hebrew woman nurse Moses. He suggested that, "She [the princess] was obliged to accept a Hebrew woman to nurse the boy, as he refused [to be nursed by] all the Egyptian women" (*Genealogical Chronology of the World Before Christ*, p. 119). No one knows if this statement is true or false. But it is intriguing.

Another question has also been raised. How long did Jochebed (the real mother of Moses) keep Moses for the nursing period?

The SDA Bible Commentary, Vol. 1, reads, "The time the child was with its mother, not stated in the Bible but given as 2 or 3 years by most commentators, was actually about 12 years" (p. 503).

From *Patriarchs and Prophets* Ellen White wrote that "She [Jochebed] kept the boy [Moses] as long as she could, but was obliged to give him up when he was about twelve years old" (p. 244).

It is clear that finding the baby in a basket on the river was no common everyday occurrence. God was definitely in charge.

2

The Key

This story may sound like fiction or a make-believe Hollywood production. It is not! Jochebed, the birth mother of Moses, is a key figure in the record of events. It is because of her teaching, training, and far-reaching influence in the first twelve years of his life that enabled Moses to become a mighty man of God.

Patriarchs and Prophets states:

> She [Jochebed] felt confident that he [Moses] had been preserved for some great work, and she knew that he must soon be given up to his royal mother, to be surrounded with influences that would tend to lead him away from God .... She endeavored to imbue [fill] his mind with the fear of God and the love of truth and justice, and earnestly prayed that he might be preserved from every corrupting influence. She showed him the folly and sin of idolatry, and early taught him to bow down and pray to the living God, who alone could hear him and help him in every emergency .... How far-reaching in its results was the influence of that one Hebrew woman, and she an exile and a slave! (pp. 243, 244).

From that same source we also read,

> By the laws of Egypt all who occupied the throne of the Pharaohs must become members of the priestly caste; and Moses, as the heir apparent, was to be initiated into the mysteries of the national religion. This duty was committed to the priests. But while he was an ardent and untiring student, he could not be induced to participate in the worship of the gods. He was threatened with the loss of the crown, and warned that he would be disowned by the princess should he persist in his adherence to the Hebrew faith.
>
> But he was unshaken in his determination to render homage to none save the one God, the Maker of heaven and earth. He reasoned with priests and worshipers, showing the folly of their superstitious veneration of senseless objects. None could refute his arguments or change his purpose, yet for the time his firmness was tolerated on account of his high position and the favor with which he was regarded by both the king and the people. (p. 245)

But what made Moses so popular with Pharaoh and the Egyptian people? Ellen White tells us why. Again, from *Patriarchs and Prophets* we read that, "At the court of Pharaoh, Moses received the highest civil and military training. The monarch had determined to make his adopted grandson his successor on

This story may sound like fiction or a make-believe Hollywood production. It is not! Jochebed, the birth mother of Moses, is a key figure in the record of events. It is because of her teaching, training, and far-reaching influence in the first twelve years of his life that enabled Moses to become a mighty man of God.

the throne, and the youth was educated for his high station .... His ability as a military leader made him a favorite with the armies of Egypt, and he was generally regarded as a remarkable character" (p. 245).

About this time, Ethiopia was engaged in a bitter war with Egypt. It continued uninterrupted for almost ten years. The Ethiopians had invaded the country and ravaged its land, including a number of cities. There was great bloodshed. But it was through Moses' leadership and training, and his position as general of the Egyptian army that drove the enemy out of the empire. He drove them back to their own capital city.

The ancient historian for Jewish history, Flavius Josephus, wrote a short, detailed account of Moses while in Ethiopia and how he found a wife there and won the war at the same time. From his book One, as translated from the Greek, Josephus gives a few details. The Ethiopian army had retreated to their royal city, Saba, the nation's capital. His account reads:

> The place was to be besieged with very great difficulty, since it was both encompassed by the Nile, and the other rivers Astapus and Astaborus, made it a very difficult thing for such as attempted to pass over them; for the city was situated in a retired place and was inhabited after the manner of an island, being encompassed with a strong wall, and having the rivers to guard them from their enemies; and having great ramparts, between the wall and the rivers, insomuch, that when the waters come with the greatest violence it can never be drowned, which ramparts make it next to impossible, for even such as have passed over the rivers, to take the city. (p. 68)

Josephus reported that Moses was upset because the Ethiopians had refused to leave their stronghold and fight. This made his army sit idle and inactive. Thus, things became stalemated. Josephus's record continues:

> Tharbis, the daughter of the king of the Ethiopians, happened to see Moses, as he led the army near the walls, and fought with

great courage; and admiring the subtlety [ability] of his undertaking, and believing him to be the author of the Egyptians' success, ... she fell deeply in love with him, and, upon the prevalency [emotion] of that passion, sent to him the most faithful of all her servants to discourse with him about marriage. (Ibid.)

Moses must have smiled, for in her suggestion of marriage he saw victory for Egypt. His answer was yes, but along with his reply was a condition. Josephus explains, "... she would procure the delivering up of the city, and gave her the assurance of an oath to take her to his wife; and that when he had once taken possession of the city, he would not break his oath to her" (Ibid.).

The report continues, "No sooner was the agreement made, but it took effect immediately; and when Moses had cut off the Ethiopians, he gave thanks to God, and ... led the Egyptians back to their land" (Ibid.).

Notice the phrase "... he [Moses] gave thanks to God" (Ibid.). This tells us quite a bit about the man, even at that time. It is commonly thought, and there is no record or proof of it, that the princess died soon after her arrival in Egypt.

That successful Ethiopian war victory also became the downfall for several other nations that had threatened Egypt's safety. As a result, Moses became a national hero. There is a very old saying, and it comes straight from the Bible. Many know it well. In Proverbs 22:6 we read, "Train up a child in the way he should go: and when he is old, he will not depart from it."

Moses is a strong example of this. He felt he was doing what God wanted him to do; however, his early training under Jochebed had not yet fully manifested itself. Given time, it would, but for the time being, he had many more lessons to learn.

My earliest boyhood memories are of living and playing in a rural-type area. There were fields to explore, fresh air to breath and Mother was always right there. Father always chose rural or quiet settings for our home.

I knew very little about the place where Father went to work every day. Its location was a long way off and a mystery to me. All I remember is that he came home late every night. It was usually long after I had gone to bed.

He owned and operated a shoe repair shop in the city of Detroit. It was located on the east side of the city in a rough neighborhood. I overheard him telling someone that in early evenings he sat by the back of his shop with the door unlocked. Why did he do this? It was because his place of business was located on a street named Myrtle, and that section of Detroit was riddled with gang warfare. It was tough and it was dangerous. I recall hearing about those street gangs such as The Purple Gang, The Black Hand, and, among others, The Myrtle Street Gang. It was a notoriously crime-ridden place and no one was safe; however, Dad knew how to handle the situation. His alert mind, knowledge of what was happening in the area and his reputation as being one of the good guys and not getting involved, plus his escape route—the unlocked door—was what protected him. This was the way he made his living. It was rough and tough, but he never brought any of its hardships home with him.

Mother, on the other hand, was a Christian woman, living in the country with my sister, Dad, and me. She was in charge at home and my father did not interfere with my upbringing. Dad never went to church. Mother did. The result! I am a Christian today because of that early, caring, God-fearing family influence, especially from Mother.

I added this record about my family for one reason. It is to demonstrate the value of early Christian training and what it did in my life. Country living, church attendance, learning from and following what the Bible teaches, even in a home with only one parent who was a devoted, practicing Christian, teaching the right principles with the complete cooperation of my father who never interfered made a lasting impression on me. I had, and still am grateful for, a mother and a father who respected each other's ways of life.

I quote again from the writings of Ellen White: "The child's first teacher is the mother. During the period of greatest susceptibility and most rapid development his education is to a great degree in her hands" (*Education*, p. 275). Thus, it was with Moses and his true mother's early training.

The first forty years in the life of Moses is almost unknown. In the palace of the Pharaoh he was trained by the best teachers ancient Egypt could offer. He grew, was protected, pampered, and surrounded by great wealth and power. But Moses had also been trained well in his beginning years. He was filled with the knowledge of the one and only true God. It never left him.

As Moses entered his forties, the training of two different ways of life clashed head-on. His deep love and strong affection for both mothers pulled him in two different directions. Emotion and loyalty ripped him apart. One offered the throne of the greatest kingdom in the then known world, the other hardship, a nation of slaves and the loss of wealth and power.

But the heart of Moses told him what to do, yet how could he do it? His Egyptian mother was fiercely loyal to him from the day she found him. Her world circled around his every move. With clever maneuvering she placed herself and him into the highest position possible. He would be Pharaoh, the king of Egypt.

Hebrews 11:24, 25 tells of his final decision. "By faith," it states, "Moses, when he was come to years, refused to be called the son of Pharaoh's daughter; choosing rather to suffer affliction with the people of God, than to enjoy the pleasures of sin for a season." Verse 27 continues. And here again we have those two words "by faith." "By faith he forsook Egypt, not fearing the wrath of the king: for he endured, as seeing him [God] who is invisible."

God won. Moses was His man.

How many hours and years did Jochebed spend in prayer for Moses? No one will ever know, but it was her and God working together that had done the job.

And what about Hatshepsut, what happened to her? We do know this much, she eventually disappeared from the pages of history. Although she was acting Pharaoh for a time, politics, intrigue, and family struggles for the throne replaced her power with a new Pharaoh.

3

He Ran

Moses quietly, and sometimes openly, attached himself to God's people, the slave nation of Israel, and whenever he visited Goshen, his faith in God grew stronger. This conviction deepened within his heart convincing him that they were indeed his own flesh and blood people.

We now have Moses, powerful in strength and in appearance. His presence automatically drew people to him. This was not of his own doing. Young and old wanted to be near him. His active, brilliant mind, impressive body and the commanding qualities of a leader demanded it. Yet, deep within himself, he knew something was missing.

What was it?

Although the hungry arms of the throne reached out to embrace him, it was not enough. Every ounce of his strength called out, "What, God? What is it? Why everything and yet nothing?" He thought he knew God. He did not. He thought he served Him. He was not. Given time, however, he would do both, for deep inside echoed a small voice and it began to grow.

You can almost imagine him looking skyward one day, and calling out, "Tell me, God, I know You are there! Help me! Who are You? Who am I, and what do You want?"

In the meantime, those close to the throne were searching for something to prove he was disloyal to Pharaoh and the Egyptian empire. Spies were everywhere watching each move he made. Finally, they rejoiced in triumph when they learned Moses had killed an Egyptian. It was common for Egyptians to use heavy sticks or rods to punish slaves, and as an Egyptian was striking the Hebrew, Moses ran to them. The Egyptian paid little or no attention to him because it was not unusual for those in authority to approve of such actions. Thus, the Egyptian kept on with his brutal attack. This is the reason why Moses was able to be close enough to the action, and in the process of stopping the attack, the Egyptian lost his life (Exod. 2:11, 12). Priests were overjoyed when they heard the news. They had proof against him. This was treason. Finally, Moses was now in their power.

Hard proof of this came the following day as two Hebrew men were fighting. Evidently Moses spent the night near Goshen, and when he witnessed the fight, he stopped it. As he did so one of the men shouted at Moses bitterly, "Who made you a prince and a judge over us?" In other words, he was pointing out that Moses was a Hebrew like them so what authority gave him, a fake Egyptian, the right to tell them what they could and could not do? (Exod. 2:14, MEV).

Then came the fatal words, "Do you intend to kill me like you killed the Egyptian?" Moses instantly froze in fear. He knew what would happen next. Once known, his enemies had their proof. He had turned against Egypt (Exod. 2:14, MEV).

This forced him to make a quick decision. He had to leave Egypt before Pharaoh got wind of it. Spies were everywhere. His life was in danger, and he knew it.

Moses was not ignorant. His training as a military leader told him that when a battle is over, especially one that failed, it called for a retreat. It was time to run. And run he did.

Moses was in panic, but not for long. Escape was his only option and only one way lay open. The desert! He could vanish into that hot, endless wasteland. No one would find him there.

He shuddered at the thought of melting into its ruthless, unyielding heart. Moses was not reckless, not for a second. No person in his right mind would hide in a fearful desert without food or water.

He knew a few Hebrews were loyal to him. His brother and sister lived in Goshen and would help. He dared not go back to the palace. News like this traveled fast.

Bible records tell us he ran (Exod. 2:15). This powerful prince of Egypt vanished into that burning wilderness.

The world's largest desert is the Sahara in North Africa. It was into this furnace that Moses made his escape. The place includes an area about one-fourth to one-third of Africa itself and stretches from the Red Sea to the Nile.

As one of the most hostile places on the planet, it fluctuates from blistering heat during daylight hours to cold, uncomfortable temperatures at night. Plant life is scarce and poorly developed. Most consist of twisted, slender stems of thorny brush. In rare places a few herbs appear. These are short-lived and blown about by wind over vast expanses of dry, hot, sandy wastes. There are few clouds, and what little rain there is usually comes from violent cloudbursts. Occasionally a natural spring will appear causing vegetation to grow. These places are called oases. They make travel possible.

It was there, in that wasteland, where Moses would begin to find God. Later in his experience, at the unexpected burning bush, he met with God. It was then that things became clearer as to why he was there. It also gave him facts and conditions concerning his future (Exod. 3).

This man had to unlearn many things, especially solving problems his own way. God was about to make drastic changes in his entire makeup.

Moses had been loved and admired as a great leader. He possessed undisputed authority and no one gave him orders. As royalty, he was obeyed without question and often took matters into his own hands. He was dependent on no one, but now all that was gone.

Moses was hunted like an animal with a price on its head. And that price was his life. Alone, battling a sea of sand and wind he was given time to reflect. Who was he anyway? Did God really select him above all others in the Hebrew nation to represent Him and to free an enslaved people? Why had he been singled out and given such high honor, glory, and responsibility to lead? And now here he was on the run, hounded in a desert wasteland. "WHY!" he cried aloud, "WHY?"

This man longed for answers. He thought he knew God, but now he realized he did not. Tears ran down his face as he searched for answers from God, the One he loved with every beat of his heart. Thus, a new life began in this man named Moses, the one who once floated on a river as a baby in a basket. However, in time, a dim light began to flicker weakly in the confused, troubled mind of this man and that light had meaning. It had understanding, and it soon grew stronger and brighter, bringing clearness and answers to this man. It would, in the future, rush over him with great force, but only when he was ready to receive it. God's time, not Moses' time, would make things clear and brilliant, bringing the Lord's unending love with abundant knowledge and purpose for the responsibility he was to receive. But for now, it was the desert, the desert only, and he was running.

He dared not travel on Egypt's network of roads across the desert. They were constantly patrolled. Ever alert, he knew those highways would be swarming with Pharaoh's soldiers. Nothing was open to him except that trackless wasteland of the Sinai Peninsula. It was all he had, and he reasoned that no one would search for him there.

Moses could not travel south or west because it all belonged to Egypt. He could not cross Egypt's eastern border into Asia either since most of it was laced with a long series of protective watchtowers. These strong, fortress-like structures were built, manned, and placed so the space between each one could be watched. No one crossed the frontier in either direction without being seen. Night crossings were possible, but dangerous. Thus, he knew he was trapped inside that vast wilderness.

Bewildered, confused, and rejected, he stumbled against blowing wind and sand. It constantly pounded every inch of his body. And each step took him closer to nowhere.

Now follows another one of those periods of time when the Bible goes silent. There is no record of his battles with the elements, or how he survived. Days and weeks were endless. There was no end as they blended into a blur of hopeless wandering. But he did survive, for the next time we find him, his head is resting on a rock pillow. He had found water, sweet, clear, cold water and there were green things to eat. With this he soon fell asleep and dreamed.

He dreamt he was listening to the quiet, soft, refreshing sound of bells, sheep, and goat bells, and he smiled. Although tired and homeless as he slept, he still smiled. Those bells were music for his tortured mind.

But those bells were not a dream. They were real, and before long, he would be hearing their comforting, gentle ring every day of his life for the next forty years. He had found a home and safety at last in a strange new land.

A text in Ezra says, "The hand of our God is upon all them for good that seek Him" (Ezra 8:22). And Moses did.

4

Teachers on Four Legs

It was no accident for Moses to find Jethro's home in Midian. Jethro was a priest and a true follower of the Hebrew God.

Deuteronomy 10:14 identifies Jethro's God. It reads, "Behold, the heaven and the heaven of heavens is the LORD's thy God, the earth also, with all that therein is." There were not many men like Jethro who believed this and, as he was soon to find out, Moses was also one of them.

But, why Jethro's house? Why was Moses guided there? God had reasons: the location was isolated, almost no one went there. The area had very little benefits to offer strangers. It was separate from the rest of the world, thus, providing an ideal place for Moses to hide.

Proof that Moses was in the right place was demonstrated at Jethro's well when Moses battled a number of menacing shepherds. The Bible account of the fight does not give how many men fought Moses. The record only states the word shepherds (Exod. 2:17). This indicates there had to be at least two. Reasonably thinking, however, one can assume there had to be more than just that amount. I say this because if it took seven women to water Jethro's animals, the threatening shepherds must have had about the same number of sheep to water or more as those in Jethro's flock. Therefore, it would take a good number of men to do the same job. Water was scarce and herds had to be driven in large numbers. This makes sense because smaller herds needed less care. It would not be worth the effort or time.

Moses also had the element of surprise on his side. The shepherds didn't even know he was there. He was outnumbered, yes, but a sudden, unexpected attack gave him the advantage. After all he was a military expert. Even then, these men were no weaklings. They lived in harsh desert lands. That took strength to survive.

No one knows how long it was before Moses arrived at the well. He had battled the elements for who knows how long and survived, only to now find himself in this fight. Weakened by the grueling condition of the desert, he fought anyway. His military training paid off as his weakened but powerful body went into action. His training was an automatic reaction which gave him unquestioned superiority. He knew how to fight. Also, his genuine compassion for others, such as the mistreatment of the women, was showing. Thus, single-handedly he drove those men away.

He then safely escorted the women home. When Jethro's daughters introduced Moses to their father, they acknowledged him as an Egyptian and he did not correct them. This was a believable assumption because in appearance he was dressed as an Egyptian, his speech, his behavior pointed that out, and besides that, his head was probably shaved as was the custom with Egyptian men. But more important to Moses, he found himself in the right place at the right time for he realized that God saw to it that he was safely hidden.

To look at Moses physically, he must have had a powerful, muscular body as well as a great mind and noble bearing. God had everything to do with the training and protection of this man, but that was not all, God had plans in mind, enormous plans, for his future.

Before Moses fled Egypt, some of the Hebrews, mostly the priesthood (elders) and even Moses himself, knew that God was to free the slaves through him. In *Patriarchs and Prophets*, Ellen White wrote an extremely important statement. It reads as follows, "The elders of Israel were taught by angels that the time for their deliverance was near, and that Moses was the man whom God would employ to accomplish this work. Angels instructed Moses also that Jehovah had chosen him to break the bondage of His people" (p. 245).

Now, here he was in exile living in a blistering desert and far from any civilization. No wonder he was confused. Did God mean what He said? He saw no way for this to happen.

Before leaving Egypt, this prediction had put Moses in a difficult position because Pharaoh, his adoptive mother, and the Egyptian people themselves all loved him. "Moses was regarded with awe by the Egyptians" (Ibid., p. 272).

After years of being pampered in the courts of Egypt and conducting highly successful military campaigns, Moses felt, or thought, that the freedom of the Hebrew nation would come through him by force and that God would be leading him down that road.

How wrong he was!

It would not happen through a show of force. It would come through a show of God's power alone. With Moses, it was as if he was trying to follow God down a one-way street and he had gone the wrong way. Something was missing here.

> *God's plans for Moses began in that homemade basket on the Nile, and now the desert had been no barrier either. The entire world belongs to God. He knows every inch of it and there was no reason, even in that wilderness waste, to change His plans or stop His leading.*

God had chosen His leader well. Moses was His man. The Lord knew him, and He also foresaw a great deal of work had to be done to prepare him before the main event could take place.

God's plans for Moses began in that homemade basket on the Nile, and now the desert had been no barrier either. The entire world belongs to God. He knows every inch of it and there was no reason, even in that wilderness waste, to change His plans or stop His leading.

In time, Moses became a working shepherd and joined the household of Jethro by marrying his daughter Zipporah.

It makes little or no difference what kind of lifestyle anyone lives, and it matters not where your home is or was. That cannot be erased from your mind because events, faces, places and things long past are forever and deeply etched into ones' memory. They will always be there, never to be erased. But God can change all that influence, good or bad, if one is willing to let Him do it. So it was with Moses in the desert home of Jethro.

Often alone, listening to the sound of sheep and goats came visions of two mothers who had often soothed his tiny hurt fingers. He remembered that both taught what is good and what is bad, each saying not to be afraid. They laughed when he laughed and dried his tears of pain by touching him with kisses of love. How could he forget such things? He never could or did.

It took forty long years as a shepherd and instruction from God, Jethro, and teachers on four legs to empty his mind of things he should forget and keep those he should. Jochebed's patience teaching the truth of who the one true God is never for a second left him. Instead, it grew stronger and more meaningful with each passing day until finally God said, "He is ready. It is time!"

Following all these years of training Moses was finally ready and willing to submit to God's commands. Forgetting much of his Egyptian background proved invaluable for his future work. But then again, and on the other hand, some of it had to be remembered.

Patriarchs and Prophets, page 251, reads:

> As the years rolled on, and he wandered with his flocks in solitary places, pondering upon the oppressed condition of his people, he recounted the dealings of God with his fathers and the promises that were the heritage of the chosen nation, and his prayers for Israel ascended by day and by night. Heavenly angels shed their light around him. Here, under the inspiration of the Holy Spirit, he wrote the book of Genesis. The long years spent amid the desert solitudes were rich in blessing, not alone to Moses and his people, but to the world in all succeeding ages.

It is of great interest to me that the ancient Egyptians probably had a written language. I grew up under the impression that hieroglyphics, a picture script showing recognizable drawings of objects such as animals, people and ordinary things was the only way the Egyptians communicated. Moses, being educated in the courts of Egypt must have learned to write and would have been skilled in its use. This is why he could write the book of Genesis and others as well. Early evidence of a written script is found in Numbers 33:2. It states that Moses, at God's request, wrote down all the travels of the Israelites from the time they left Egypt until they reached the Jordan River facing the city of Jericho.

One more observation. Moses, in order to write the history of the Hebrews in the book of Genesis, had to know that history before writing it down. I believe his source material for that writing must have come from several places. First, his birth mother Jochebed, and maybe others around her, then later from his father-in-law Jethro. All were rich in Hebrew history. Again, this speaks well of a mother's early training. Young minds retain such things, and Moses did just that. He remembered. Greatest of all, he was inspired and given information from God Himself through the Holy Spirit.

It seems forever before this runaway prince of Egypt turned shepherd, was ready to stand face to face with a tree, or as the Bible states, a bush that was on fire and would not burn.

It was then, at long last, at that fiery bush that Moses had finally become completely submissive to God's leading. His direct contact with the God he deeply loved, respected and served began to unfold, showing him the work he was born to do.

5

Those Forty Long Years

Let's pause for a moment.

Here we have a man. A man named Moses. He was far from home and living in a foreign land named Midian. He had changed palace walls for towering rock formations. Polished floors were now rolling hills of sand, and his loyal troops were sheep and goats. Instead of riding in chariots, he walked in sandals. The proud staff of authority he once carried became a shepherd's rod and instead of magnificent robes of state and shining armor, he dressed in rough, homespun wool.

A princess, his adoring, adoptive mother, even the admiration of the Pharaoh himself, king of the most powerful nation on earth, were gone forever.

Every organization, ancient or new, have top executives. Egypt was no exception. Moses had been one step away from a top position. He would have been Pharaoh but for one very important factor. *God said no.*

His fall had been earth-shaking and left him broken and shattered. He had nothing to offer his new home or Jethro. From fame and fortune to a place in a stranger's home is all there was. Thus, Moses offered himself for hire. How else could he earn room and board? Jethro took him up on the deal. Moses could stay and work as a shepherd for as long as he wanted to.

And stay he did.

But, what kind of work does a shepherd do? He had no idea. *Oh!* he thought, *How did I get into this?* Facing no other option, Moses accepted the job. Instead of hordes of bowing servants, his subjects became living and breathing creatures on four legs, and seven women, Jethro's daughters, were his willing teachers.

First lesson: sheep require about one and a half gallons of water every day. Snow or dew help, but there was little or none of either one of those. This was the main reason for Jethro's well. How was he to get those creatures to that well? Animals such as these were not allowed to travel more than two miles in hot weather, and there was nothing but hot weather. Gleefully, those seven women were more than happy to show him the answer. And there was much more to learn.

Sheep need shade from the burning sun because of their thick wool. There were predators they needed protection from including men, wolves, lions and even eagles. What about the problem of urging animals to mate, or not to? It was common and accepted knowledge for one ram to have many ewes. How could he handle that?

Problems, problems, problems!

The primary reason for raising sheep was twofold: meat and wool, and possibly milk. Flocks had to be healthy. Watching for sickness or disease, and recognizing the symptoms was essential. What about broken legs, stray, or lost animals? Would he ever learn? Could he learn? And the goats were a real problem! He didn't even want to think about them.

Range goats were treated differently from pastured goats. They had to be kept completely dry because of their long hair. They also had to be moved to different areas often to prevent disease. That, and tending sheep, was an entirely new and different way of life. Could he handle it? He just gulped, sighed, took a deep breath, and started in.

The palace, with all its internal and political intrigue, never looked better to him than it did now. But there was no turning back even if he wanted to, and he didn't want to. God led him there and he knew it.

Did desert winds laugh at Moses? Did the crunch of sand whisper beneath his feet, reminding him of servants, fine food, wealth, lost glory, great power and more? Did all this rush back haunting his every waking hour? Did the helpless cries and hopeless tears of forsaken slaves reach across desert sands to pound in his ears?

One purpose for this study is to take a strong look at an unusual human being. He did live thousands of years ago, and for us to be able to sit across from him and ask questions is not an option. Yet, there are records, as we have already discovered, and it is from these that we get a limited, realistic insight. To discover how God led and planned the events of his life may hopefully explain unanswered questions as to the how and why God works in the lives of you and me, that is, if we allow Him to do so.

Was Moses lonesome for Egypt? After all, he grew up there. We have a clue, and it is found in Exodus 2:22, "And she [Moses' wife Zipporah] bare him a son, and he called his name Gershom: for he said, I have been a stranger in a strange land."

The SDA Bible Commentary, vol. 1, page 506, has this explanation for the name Gershom: "Moses explains the name by referring to the fact that he was a stranger in a strange land. Though he had saved his life, he was living in exile, and gave expression to his feeling of loneliness and humiliation in naming his first son."

Forty years is a long time to forget one's past. Once, long ago, God had spoken to him as being the promised deliverer for His people. It had not happened! He was now married, with children, living under the roof of his father-in-law and he had a seemingly ordinary job as a simple shepherd. He was considered a nobody. So, where was the fulfillment of God's promise?

Humiliated and embarrassed, he felt the heavy weight of both backgrounds. How else could he feel about those he left behind plus his present situation? Everything and everyone he knew before now was in Egypt, his foster mother, his real mother, their years of love and devotion. Each in their own way had stood up for him while others did not. All their hopes, training and ambitions had centered on him. He felt he had failed them both.

Then too, was he thinking of the pride of past accomplishments? If so, what good were they to him now, and, what about the Hebrew elders? What were they thinking about this runaway deliverer? Were they wondering if he was even alive? Thus, because of him their faith in God had to be under great stress.

Moses felt his shame and it hurt. Regret, anger, remorse, loneliness—he felt it all. He was nothing but a broken failure, an impoverished man without a future. Sheep, goats, strangers, and an unrelenting, merciless, pitiless desert was all he had. Was this the promised kingdom?

The feelings of Moses demonstrate that he was just like us with all the same thoughts and mindsets as you and I have. He was just one more frustrated human being except for one thing—he was in love with God.

Can we say with Moses that "... the peace of God, which passeth all understanding, shall keep your hearts and minds through Christ Jesus" (Phil. 4:7)?

We can and we should!

6

It Didn't Burn

Desert growth is not like those where water and rain are plentiful. Trees, as most of us know, do not grow in dry sand, except on an oasis. And when oasis trees do grow, they are usually tall, un-branched palms with a crown of leaves at the top. What Moses was seeing every day was a bush-like growth.

Year after year, as he wandered from place to place with his flocks and herds, he became familiar with this bleak, harsh surrounding. It's a strange beauty and the stillness became normal to him. All this was changing his entire outlook. Caring for sheep and goats taught him many things. One was patience, another was to accept things as they were. His wooly charges gave him many insights. He learned the meaning of caring, trust, dependence, tenderness, protection, healing and how to defend. He began to guide instead of issuing orders and commands.

God was shaping this man for the leadership role He was soon to place on him. Yet his past skills of strong leadership, authority and responsibility in Egypt were also to become essential for his future. But these abilities had to be refined and take on a different nature if he was to use them for guiding people out of bondage.

Was he ready for it? He didn't know. How could he? But he and a nation of slaves were about to find out.

Now we come to the bush that refused to burn. Some say it was a tree and not a bush, but whatever it was, let's take a look at it.

As Moses moved his charges to the west of Jethro's home and up the slopes of Mount Horeb "... the angel of the LORD appeared unto him in a flame of fire out of the midst of a bush: and he looked, and, behold, the bush burned with fire, and the bush was not consumed" (Exod. 3:2).

Moses had seen many strange and unusual sights in the desert. Most were shrugged off as not important; however, this was not normal. Curiosity held his attention as he decided to take a closer look.

The bush was indeed on fire, but its leaves, branches and the entire plant never changed. It was never consumed. Other bushes were nearby, but this one was the only one on fire. Fascinated, he walked closer.

Suddenly he tensed up. Someone was calling his name. He looked around. No one was there. "Don't come any closer," the voice said (Exod. 3:5, TLB). Not yet aware of God's presence, he stopped, stayed a safe distance from this great wonder and waited.

The voice spoke again, only stronger this time and more direct. There came an order, a command, "Take off your shoes, for you are standing on holy ground" (Exod. 3:5, TLB).

Those words from that powerful and invisible Someone was coming from inside that fire. Going to his knees, Moses, without uttering a sound or looking up, nervously removed his sandals. In that part of the world it was considered sacrilegious to go into a clean or holy place with shoes on. It would contaminate the place if one's shoes were not removed.

Light from the fire grew intensely bright, but it didn't flare or burn up. It just flamed as the voice identified Itself. Moses covered his face and head as the voice continued, "I am the God of thy father," it continued, "the God of Abraham, the God of Isaac, and the God of Jacob" (Exod. 3:6).

God assured Moses that He was well aware of what was happening to the Hebrew slaves in Egypt. "I have surely seen the affliction of my people which are in Egypt, and have heard their cry by reason of their taskmasters; for I know their sorrows" (Exod. 3:7). Moses dared not speak. He just listened.

Quoting from Exodus 3:8, 9, we read God's next words concerning the Hebrews:

> And I am come down to deliver them out of the hand of the Egyptians, and to bring them up out of that land unto a good land and a large, unto a land flowing with milk and honey; unto the place of the Canaanites, and the Hittites, and the Amorites, and the Perizzites, and the Hivites, and the Jebusites. Now therefore, behold, the cry of the children of Israel is come unto me: and I have also seen the oppression wherewith the Egyptians oppress them.

The next words God uttered threw Moses into a cold sweat. He trembled with fear. For God said, "Come now therefore, and I will send thee unto Pharaoh, that thou mayest bring forth my people the children of Israel out of Egypt" (Exod. 3:10).

What would you do if you heard such words? What could you say, if anything, if God suddenly decided to speak to you one on one?

He can do it. He knows exactly who and where you are at all times. God knows what you say, how you act, even what you think—bald or not. Matthew 10:30 says "... the very hairs of your head are all numbered."

God called Moses by his own name and He knows yours too. Filled with awe, terror and hardly able to speak, Moses finally managed, in a frightened voice, to stutter a few words. I feel sure it was almost a whisper as he said, "Who am I that I should go to Pharaoh ...?" (Exod. 3:11, RSV).

Moses was ready to do as God asked, but he didn't know it yet. This meeting with God scared him. That once-powerful prince of Egypt was now a thing of the past.

"The fact that a man feels his weakness is at least some evidence that he realizes the magnitude of the work appointed him, and that he will make God his counselor and his strength" (*Patriarchs and Prophets*, p. 255).

"Who am I?" Moses asked. That was not all Moses said. His complete words were, "Who am I, that I should go unto Pharaoh, and that I should bring forth the children of Israel out of Egypt?" (Exod. 3:11)

After the initial shock of being in God's presence began to decrease somewhat, God and Moses began talking more openly and a strong bond of closeness began to build. Moses had many excuses why he was not able to do what God wanted him to do.

From that moment on, God slowly revealed His plans for rescuing His people. Instructions were given to Moses about his future role as leader of the Hebrew nation. Detail after detail was revealed, the good as well as the bad. Strategy, the entire plan, Pharaoh's reaction, and future events were explained. God also stated that further instructions would be given as the events took place. Basically, there would be no surprises. Moses was shocked and overwhelmed. Dare he ask more questions? (*Patriarchs and Prophets*, p. 253).

Exodus 4:10 reveals something startling. As an honored member of Egypt's royal family, Moses was well-schooled and elegant in speech. But now because of those forty years of lonely desert wanderings, with only animals for company, he had lost most of his refined, dignified tastes, training, and style, especially his polished ability to speak. Moses not only listened to God; he was slow to speak. It took courage to say anything. He finally called out, "O my LORD ... I am slow of speech, and of a slow tongue" (Exod. 4:10).

I think this pleased God for He answered, "Who hath made man's mouth? or who maketh the dumb, or deaf, or the seeing, or the blind? have not I the Lord? Now therefore go, and I will be with thy mouth, and teach thee what thou shalt say" (Exod. 4:11, 12).

Moses was not happy with this arrangement and said so. At last God had enough of his weak excuses. He knew Moses was the man for the job because He had been training him to do it for years. Verse 14 reads, "And the anger of the LORD was kindled against Moses" (Exod. 4:14).

This statement is strong, and I believe God's reaction was that He was displeased. It appeared as if Moses was looking for excuses to back out from what God was asking. God knows us and our excuses too!

But God knew Moses. He was well aware of this man's ways and had already solved the slow speech problem by sending Aaron to him. His brother Aaron was already on his way to join Moses. In reality, what God was saying to Moses was, "Wake up, face it, trust Me and don't be like that, for I already told you I would be with you. You are not alone."

There was no question about the loyalty of Moses to God. The Lord knew that. Instead, on the part of Moses, it was a matter of shock. But God chose well. Moses was capable of doing the job. It was only a matter of convincing him. Verse 14 went on to solve the fears and excuses of Moses. God asked, "Is not Aaron the Levite thy brother?" (Exod. 4:14). He continued, "I know that he can speak well. And also, behold, he cometh forth to meet thee: and when he seeth thee, he will be glad in his heart. And thou shalt speak unto him, and put words in his mouth: and I will be with thy mouth, and with his mouth, and will teach you what ye shall do" (Exod. 4:14, 15).

This ended the conversation at the burning bush. From that minute on Moses was God's chosen deliverer for the Israelites. Without question, Moses was now ready and willing to trust God by agreeing to whatever the Lord asked of him.

Should we do less?

7

He Went

Following the intense meeting with God, there was not much sleep in Jethro's house that night. Moses, with his father-in-law, must have talked far into the early sunrise hours of the next morning. Jethro finally said, "Go in peace" (Exod. 4:18, RSV).

"A secret dread of Pharaoh and the Egyptians, whose anger had been kindled against him forty years before, had rendered Moses still more reluctant to return to Egypt; but after he had set out to obey the divine command, the Lord revealed to him that his enemies were dead" (*Patriarchs and Prophets*, p. 255).

Notice the words "after he had set out to obey." This speaks of action, proof of one's willingness to obey, no matter the outcome. He went!

As he traveled toward Egypt, important information came to him from his meeting with God at the fiery bush. It involved idol or image-making, for when the bush was burning, and God's voice spoke from its center, no visible form appeared. Deuteronomy 4:15 reads "... ye saw no manner of similitude [image or likeness of anything] on the day that the Lord spake unto you in Horeb out of the midst of the fire."

"Man is prone to seek to express his concepts of deity in visible, material form. The manifestation of divine glory at Sinai was not to be an excuse for doing so" (*The SDA Bible Commentary*, vol. 1, p. 968).

This is why God sometimes hides Himself in such things as the brightness of light or fire. The pillar of fire leading the Hebrews and Paul's bright light on the Damascus road are but two such examples. A large section of Deuteronomy 4 explains this.

The Ten Commandments themselves make it very plain that nothing made by man's hands should ever be worshiped as a god. Yet, people continually do this forbidden act in one form or another. Ancient Egypt was a prime example for this. Moses was raised in its idol-worship environment. And again, if it were not for his real mother, Jochebed, he would have followed in the ways and beliefs of his adopted Egyptian heritage.

Now, Moses was going back to Egypt, not as a cherished and pampered prince, but as a true believer in the God of heaven and earth. He was nervous, and somewhat fearful, and this was normal, but there was no thought of turning back. God had spoken, and regardless of what lay ahead, Moses was going where God was leading him.

He met his brother Aaron in the desert, and what a happy reunion that was. They even wept for joy when they first sighted each other. They walked then ran, almost flying into each other's arms. Finally, there in that barren wasteland, the two brothers, alone yet together, excitedly told each other what God had said and done to and for each other through all those forty long, lonely years. They became emotional and nervous all at the same time. Next they prayed together committing themselves to what God was asking them, especially Moses, to do. They pleaded for His care and guidance.

The next step was to return to Egypt and the Hebrew nation at Goshen. First, however, Moses thought of his immediate family, his wife, and sons. They must go with him. But this did not happen. They started for Egypt as a family, but Moses was impressed to send them back to stay with his father-in-law, Jethro. He knew this was best because of the tremendous hardships ahead. Besides, they might be a stumbling block for him in the work God was directing him to do. He needed a clear mind for this work. He and God must work together without extra burdens such as caring for a family. The thought could also have come to him that the

Egyptians could use his family as leverage to stop his work. Thus, it was best not only for what lay ahead, but also for their safety and his as well. He was a good father and husband, but deep within his heart, God came first. Nothing must interfere with that (*Patriarchs and Prophets*, p. 383).

Now, the way was open for both him and Aaron to make the trip to Egypt together with God. Things happened fast once the brothers arrived in Egypt. The first stop was Goshen.

Unauthorized to do so, they called for the elders and leading men of Israel to assemble before them. This was done. One reason they complied to Moses' command was that God had told Moses to do this, and they believed him. Moses and Aaron called for reform.

In their long years as a nation of slaves, most Israelites lost touch with or knew very little about God's law. The Sabbath in particular had almost been done away with. They said it could not be observed because of their supervisors, the Egyptian taskmasters as the Bible calls them. They made them work every day. Even then there were loyal believers, men and women who stood fast to the worship of God.

> [They] were sorely troubled as they saw their children daily witnessing [watching] the abominations of the heathen, and even bowing down to their false gods …. They did not conceal their faith, but declared to the Egyptians that the object of their worship was the Maker of heaven and earth, the only true and living God. They rehearsed the evidences of His existence and power, from creation down to the days of Jacob. The Egyptians thus had an opportunity to become acquainted with the religion of the Hebrews. (*Patriarchs and Prophets*, p. 259)

Most Egyptians laughed at them for their strange beliefs by saying, "What can slaves know about God??" They tried to change their Israelite ways with bribes, and when that didn't work, there were threats. Next was harsh, cruel treatment. As a result of the arrival and influence of Moses and Aaron, and the elders backing them up, the Hebrews kept Sabbath and there was a massive work shortage in Egypt (*Patriarchs and Prophets*, p. 259).

Pharaoh was furious when he heard about it. He feared an uprising or worse yet, war. His answer to what he called their so-called threat was more and harder work, especially on that Sabbath of theirs. Thus, when the shortage of bricks began to show up, Hebrew officers acting as bosses under the direction of taskmasters, were brutally beaten. Moses was blamed for all of this.

Many of the Egyptians were making jests and fun of this make-believe God of the Hebrews. They scornfully and sarcastically said, "If your God is just and merciful, and possesses power above that of the Egyptian gods, why does He not make you a free people?" (Ibid.).

They declared that their gods had given the Hebrews to them as slaves, and that no God of the Hebrews, whoever He might be, could take them away from them.

This was devastating to the Israelite people. It demoralized and totally discouraged most of the nation. Something had to be done—and soon.

Moses called the people together in Goshen and repeated God's promise of freedom to them and God's planned future for giving them a land of their own. They did not believe him. Slavery had taken its toll on their belief in God.

Moses and Aaron assembled the elders and important leaders together for prayer. He was going to see the Pharaoh who had forgotten that Moses had once been a courtier himself holding a high position in the kingdom. Moses knew how to get that forbidden access.

All foreign ambassadors, officially representing other nations had no access to the Pharaoh unless summoned. No one, said the elders, was allowed access to him.

Moses must have smiled at this because he knew of a way to do it. Most had ready access to Pharaoh with bribes or by offering rich gifts. Moses would do none of that.

In spite of open doubt, Moses, taking matters into his own hands, decided to break the rules. And when he did, he would ask Pharaoh to let God's people go. Most leaders thought this request was doomed to fail. But Moses, regardless of what they were saying, and with God's help, would go to Pharaoh with his brother. Whatever the outcome, the interview would be in God's hands.

Taking Aaron with him, they went to the palace and were announced as the official representatives of the great King of the universe, the King of kings, Jehovah. As a result, they were formally ushered into the presence of Pharaoh.

Following diplomatic formality and introductions, they humbly announced they were speaking on behalf of Jehovah, and that His words, as spoken through them, were these, "'Thus saith Jehovah, God of Israel, Let My people go, that they may hold a feast unto Me in the wilderness.' 'Who is Jehovah, that I should obey His voice to let Israel go?' demanded the monarch; 'I know not Jehovah, neither will I let Israel go'" (Ibid., p. 257).

Moses was not afraid of this man or his threats as he called out, "The God of the Hebrews hath met with us: let us go, we pray thee, three days' journey into the desert, and sacrifice unto the Lord our God; lest He fall upon us with pestilence, or with the sword" (Ibid.).

Rumors had reached the king that this, a ridiculous request, would be presented. It was also reported as nothing more than a cover-up for a revolt. Pharaoh knew about the work of Moses among the Hebrews and he was advised that this man and his brother Aaron were stirring up trouble among his slaves and that the movement they began was spreading rapidly.

Pharaoh would have nothing to do with this request and ordered both Moses and Aaron out of his sight. As they were leaving, they overheard Pharaoh giving additional instructions and orders. He said that because of these two men, work had stopped on their so-called Sabbath which had slowed the daily production of building bricks. He ordered that this had to end. As punishment for this action against him, he commanded the Israelites to continue supplying the same daily number of bricks, but they would from then on gather their own straw, a vital ingredient for making bricks.

Egypt would no longer supply that need. This meant more than twice as much work for the slaves. They began to panic and complain violently.

One reason that the Egyptians were against this three-day trip into the wilderness was because there would be animal sacrifices to God, and some of the animals to be offered were sacred to the Egyptians. It would be offensive to them for this to happen.

Thus, the war, which started in heaven between God and Satan, began to intensify. It was not a war with men destroying one another physically, or by weapons that wound and kill. Instead, it was a deadly conflict and a bitterly decisive one between principalities and powers.

Once again, we find Moses in the middle of an impossible situation. The Hebrews blamed him for their added misery, the Egyptians were making fun of him and his God and Pharaoh was refusing to budge.

It was time for God to step in, but before He did, *Patriarchs and Prophets* states, "The Lord directed Moses to go again to the people and repeat the promise of deliverance, with a fresh assurance of divine favor. He went as he was commanded; but they would not listen" (p. 260).

Following this, God asked Moses to return to Pharaoh, asking once again to let the slaves go. What was the reaction? "In discouragement [he was human] he replied, 'Behold, the children of Israel have not harkened unto me; how then shall Pharaoh hear me?' He was told to take Aaron with him and go before Pharaoh, and again demand 'that he send the children of Israel out of his land'" (Ibid., p. 263).

Even after all the signs and wonders he performed for the king, like his rod turning into a snake, plus other wonders, Moses hesitated to go. Why? Because Pharaoh was not impressed by what he did through God's power, so why, he reasoned, would he listen now and let the Israelites go?

God replied to his thinking by saying that the "monarch would not yield until God should visit judgments upon Egypt and bring out Israel" (Ibid.). Moses went, but after his appearance Pharaoh still would not budge or release the slaves.

God delayed judgments for a time because "The Lord would give the Egyptians an opportunity to see how vain was the wisdom of their mighty men, how feeble the power of their gods ... He would punish the people of Egypt for their idolatry and silence their boasting of the blessings received from their senseless deities. God would glorify His own name that other nations might hear of His power and tremble" (Ibid.).

Most of the Israelites were worshiping idols as the Egyptians did. Thus, God was also giving the Hebrew nation time to return to Him that they "... might be led to turn from their idolatry and render Him pure worship" (Ibid.).

Idols come in different forms even today. Police courts testify to that every day that people have made idols of alcohol, drugs, money, and power. Many Christians practice idol worship by their actions and lifestyles.

Hopefully, none of this can be found among God's true followers, but sadly it is growing.

8

God's Amazing Weapons

Following the failed meeting with Pharaoh, and the demonstrations of Moses' rod with its miracles, God told Moses what he should do next.

Pharaoh had a habit of bathing in the Nile River every morning. This was also a physical sign showing that he worshiped the river god. The morning following the meeting with Pharaoh, Moses and Aaron appeared at the river as the king arrived.

Speaking directly to Pharaoh, Moses informed him that "The LORD God of the Hebrews hath sent me unto thee, saying, Let my people go, that they may serve me in the wilderness: and, behold, hitherto thou wouldest not hear. Thus saith the LORD, In this thou shalt know that I am the LORD: behold, I will smite with the rod that is in mine hand upon the waters which are in the river, and they shall be turned to blood" (Exod. 7:16, 17). Ignoring Moses, Pharaoh stepped into the water. What was the result?

Aaron also stretched his rod above the water and the water turned red like blood (Exod. 7:20). The Nile's water took on a heavier appearance than normal water quality. It thickened, then spread rapidly to as far as the eye could see. Pharaoh shuddered and became nervous, not believing what he saw.

Magicians ran to his rescue by also producing a red substance in water (Exod. 7:22). But it was not blood. Pharaoh's glaring eyes and pompous attitude returned. "A trick," he uttered. "It's all a trick," he roared as he and his court stalked off. "Moses is playing tricks again. There is no god but ours."

A remarkable truth about Pharaoh's magicians comes from Ellen White. In her book *Patriarchs and Prophets* she says:

> But the prince of evil had a still deeper object in manifesting his wonders through the magicians. He well knew that Moses, in breaking the yoke of bondage from off the children of Israel, pre-figured [represented] Christ, who was to break the reign of sin over the human family. He knew that when Christ should appear, mighty miracles would be wrought [produced] as an evidence to the world that God had sent Him. Satan trembled for his power. By counterfeiting the work of God through Moses, he hoped not only to prevent the deliverance of Israel, but to exert an influence through future ages to destroy faith in the miracles of Christ. Satan is constantly seeking to counterfeit the work of Christ and to establish his own power and claims. He leads men to account for the miracles of Christ by making them appear to be the result of human skill and power. In many minds he thus destroys faith in Christ as the Son of God, and leads them to reject the gracious offers of mercy through the plan of redemption. (pp. 264, 265)

The blood spread quickly across the river. Side streams and other flowing bodies of water, even pools were filled with it. Every bit of water in sight was filled with blood. Dead fish floated to the surface of rivers and streams.

As time continued, an ugly, rotting odor emerged. The stench of decaying fish and stale blood filled the air in every direction. Days passed as animals and people searched and cried aloud for water, especially children. Men, women, boys, and girls began digging in the ground in search of water to drink.

Pharaoh was hounded constantly. *"Water!"* was all he heard. "Give us water or we will die!"

Pharaoh's magicians were able to create what looked like blood from water, but try as they may, they could not reverse the process. Six days passed but when the seventh day of the plague ended, and fresh water returned, Moses returned, and with a strong voice demanded, "The Lord God says, let my people go!" Pharaoh's heart was hardened. He could do nothing except yell, "Go, all of you. Go!" The Hebrew slaves were to remain and continue as before.

Frogs were sacred to the Egyptians and they worshiped a frog-headed goddess who, they thought, possessed creative power. One reason for God choosing frogs as one of the plagues was to show how foolish it was to devote themselves to such a repulsive creature.

In the first of the calamities, the gruesome upheaval of blood, his magicians were able to simulate the bloody water and Pharaoh's heart was hardened (Exod. 22:7). In his arrogance, he never learned the lesson of his folly. As a result, each succeeding plague grew in intensity and became more lethal than the previous ones.

So, frogs were next. They were everywhere in great numbers, on streets, in homes, closets, temples, palaces, bedrooms. No place was without hordes of frogs. They were stepped on, shoveled aside, killed, and burned in piles. There was no end of them, and they grew greater in number every minute of every hour.

Pharaoh himself was tormented. He could not sleep because of their constant croaking. Worse yet, those clammy, slimy creatures filled his bed. The frog god became hated. Obliged to respect and love this goddess, the people now hated all she stood for. She had spitefully betrayed them.

Once again Pharaoh's magicians stepped in. They played tricks on the king by giving him the illusion of creating frogs. When asked to get rid of those creatures they could not do it.

Pharaoh immediately gave in and called for Moses and Aaron, pleading with them to ask their Hebrew God for help. Moses prayed, and God took the frogs away (Exod. 8:8–13).

Pharaoh, either insane or drunk with power, thinking there would be no more plagues, refused again to let the Hebrews go.

The plagues lasted for an estimated period of six months, possibly longer. There were ten in all, striking directly at Egypt's false religion, fake gods, and so-called deities. It was God's plan to convince these people that there is no other god but Him.

Stronger disasters were to follow the frogs, and as the Lord informed Moses of their nature he, in time, instructed Pharaoh of their devastation and the consequences. These warnings were to give the monarch time to choose not only to save himself but his subjects as well from the deadly results.

Moses always prayed before going to Pharaoh. His long years as a shepherd taught him the value of relying completely on God, and prayer was the key to his success in whatever he did. The solitude of those years gave him the will and the power to depend on God and God only. Thus, he prayed.

"The fact that a man feels his weakness [as Moses did] is at least some evidence that he realizes the magnitude of the work appointed him, and that he will make God his counselor and his strength" (Ibid., p. 255). Here was a man in love with God.

The warnings from God to Pharaoh through Moses and Aaron were as clear as ever. Let my people go! Other warnings were also spoken to Pharaoh with added advice of caution against his repeated stubbornness and ego. The king was outraged. No shepherd tells Pharaoh what to do. Thus, he kept the Hebrews in check. They would remain as slaves.

One morning as the king bathed in the Nile, Moses and Aaron appeared again. At God's command Aaron lifted his hand and lice covered all of Egypt.

And so it went. Plague followed plague and the king constantly changed his decision from yes to no.

Egyptians, the king's counselors, even court magicians pled with Pharaoh to let the slaves, the Israelites go. All agreed that the Hebrew God was the only God, and the idols they worshiped were nothing but fakes.

"Then Pharaoh's servants said to him, 'How long shall this man [Moses] be a snare to us? Let the men go, so that they may serve the LORD their God. Do you not yet know that Egypt is destroyed?'" (Exod. 10:7, MEV).

The stubborn king was Satan's key weapon. Although he knew the battle was lost, Satan continued to fight as innocent people suffered and died. "Not yet," both Pharaoh and Satan called out, "NO! The fight is not over."

"Thus far the courtiers [of Pharaoh] seem not to have ventured their own opinion, at least in opposition to Pharaoh. Except for the magicians, who had pointed to the lice of the third plague as the finger of God .... But now they speak forth their fears, ... they became genuinely alarmed, fearing that further calamities would ruin them permanently" (*The SDA Bible Commentary*, vol. 1, pp. 542, 543).

In spite of all their fears, Pharaoh remained stubborn and unmoving as ever. He was Satan's man, and the plagues continued to fall.

"In the plagues that fell upon Egypt we behold a preview of the more terrible and extensive judgments of God soon to fall upon the earth" (Ibid., p. 529).

9

A Strange Dinner

> God speaks to men through His servants, giving cautions and warnings, and rebuking sin. He gives to each an opportunity to correct his errors before they become fixed in the character; but if one refuses to be corrected, divine power does not interpose to counteract the tendency of his own action. He finds it more easy to repeat the same course. He is hardening the heart against the influence of the Holy Spirit. A further rejection of light places him where a far stronger influence will be ineffectual to make an abiding impression. (*Patriarchs and Prophets*, p. 268)

Goshen, where the Hebrews lived, was not touched by the devastating plagues that practically ruined the rest of the nation. These were God's chosen people. A few of Pharaoh's courtiers began to realize this. Although seemingly loyal to the king, they began to wonder about Moses and his God.

As stated, there was always a warning to Pharaoh before each plague took place. A number of Pharaoh's courtiers, called servants, acted upon the warnings of Moses. "He that feared the word of the LORD among the servants [officials] of Pharaoh made his servants and his livestock flee into the houses [shelters, barns, and other structures]" (Exod. 9:20, MEV).

So, when the storm broke at the seventh plague with fire, wind and hail they, along with their servants and cattle, were safe.

From *The SDA Bible Commentary*, vol. 1, page 538, we find this reference: "For the first time an intimation is made that there were Egyptians who had learned to fear [reverence] the Lord. Apparently the effect of the plagues had gradually convinced many of them that the God of the Hebrews was indeed a powerful God .... At the Exodus a mixed multitude apparently not Hebrews themselves left Egypt with the departing slaves."

What does the phrase "And God hardened Pharaoh's heart" mean? These words do not explain the way God influences or works in the hearts and minds of people. So, what does that phrase mean?

When someone sins, God will point to his or her wrong actions or way of thinking. He does it in several ways. He may do it through friends, circumstances, family, Bible study or in other countless ways. As a result, that person may react in one of two ways. One, he may accept His warning and correct his ways. Or two, he will reject His cautions and continue doing what is known to be wrong. Therefore, if someone repeatedly rejects God's counsel and continues his or her old ways and habits, the Lord may point them out even stronger.

But if a person continues rejecting the counsel, it will often deepen their mind to continue their wrongdoing. This hardens one's heart toward God. Thus, they do it to themselves. The Lord will never interfere with anyone's decision. The choice is theirs. But even then, He will not give up working with the person who chooses wrong. He will continue to give them time and every opportunity to change until they finally and completely say NO and reject His counsel and pleading completely. This is one reason for the trouble we sometimes shrug off and blame God for. Ego is involved here.

As the plagues increased in strength, they also came closer together. Pharaoh realized this. At the same time his mind became increasingly hard. Being the clever man that he was, he also used Moses and the knowledge of his God to his advantage. He switched from time to time between plagues. When the plague became more powerful, he called for Moses, admitting he had done wrong and that the God of Moses was the true God. He would then ask Moses to stop the plague and if he would do so, he promised to release the Israelites to go and worship their God. Notice he said their God, not his.

Without realizing it he was admitting that the God of the Israelites was the only God, and the ones he served were manmade objects and not gods at all.

"As he [Pharaoh] continued to venture on in his own course, going from one degree of stubbornness to another, his heart became more and more hardened [rigid], until he was called to look upon the cold, dead faces of the first-born" (*Patriarchs and Prophets*, p. 268). That included his own son, the crown prince.

The people of Egypt now began to think of Moses as a god just as they did Pharaoh. They witnessed every devastating plague and since Moses was associated with them, they reverenced him.

Each plague so far involved some form of nature and since the Egyptians worshiped nature as gods, they firmly believed that the God of Moses had complete control even over their own deities. Although they held Moses in awe, they were afraid of him and would welcome the prospect of him and the Israelites moving out of their country.

When God told the Hebrew nation, through Moses, to ask their Egyptian neighbors for valuables, the Egyptians never hesitated. This was to be in partial recompense for all their unpaid labors. The Egyptians willingly gave their treasures, gold, silver, precious stones and jewelry, anything and everything they asked for. They were too scared of what might happen to refuse (*Patriarchs and Prophets*, p. 281, and Exod. 11:2).

Moses also informed the Israelites to be ready for a special feast called the Passover. Certain lambs were to be chosen for that event and when it came time to prepare them for eating, they were to take the animal's blood and brush it on their doorpost, including the area above the door.

The reason for this was when the time came for the angel of death to come to Egypt, he would pass over every home that had blood on the doorposts and all those inside the building would be safe. This was the final plague. If there was no blood on the doorposts the firstborn of each household, including Pharaoh and the animals, would all die.

The war between God and Satan had intensified. It was in crisis now and the Lord was ready and about to perform His last drastic maneuver in Egypt. God had plans for His people. He had singled them out from the millions of earth's population to proclaim who He was. They had the truth and were chosen to be His priests, His representatives, to inform the entire world about Him and why they were living on the earth.

Although the Hebrew nation was destined to be His chosen ambassadors, Satan knew it too and he was doing his best to prevent its truth, its purpose, and its mission from spreading. Thus, the war continued. The battle lines were in place. On one side the Israelites were prepared and ready, and on the other Pharaoh and the devil were also ready and equipped for battle. Yet one major difference lay between the two sides—the Lord was in control.

In Goshen, the special feast had been eaten, blood was in place, and now they waited the outcome in silence with their greatest weapon on hand and in place—prayer.

10

Go

God had a message for the Israelites through that meal of lamb which had to be eaten quickly. Exodus 12:11, 12 tells why it was so special. Verse 11 explains, "And thus shall ye eat it; with your loins girded [clothes on], your shoes on your feet, and your staff in your hand; and ye shall eat it in haste: it is the LORD's passover." Verse 12 continues "For I will pass through the land of Egypt this night, and will smite all the firstborn in the land of Egypt, both man and beast; and against all the gods of Egypt I will execute judgment: I am the LORD."

This message would save their lives.

God told Moses earlier that Pharaoh would never change his attitude no matter what He (God through Moses) said or promised. Now the Lord fulfilled His Word about the firstborn.

When God told Moses of His plan it did two things. The first is that Moses always knew ahead of time what Pharaoh would say and do. This helped him not to be discouraged, which had happened in times past. There would be no surprises for God's actions. And second, it taught him patience and tolerance.

Today we call this understanding. Moses certainly needed this when dealing with Pharaoh. Moses was ready for anything God did or had in mind. Having this direct contact with God, Moses had an advantage over the king as he continued to work as long as he did, hoping for a change in the attitude of Pharaoh and his subjects.

"... [I]t was ever God's purpose to teach men to recognize Him, not as a local god, [as the Egyptians were doing] but as the ruler of heaven and earth" (*The SDA Bible Commentary*, vol. 7, p. 539).

Ellen White makes this clear. She wrote:

> God's judgments will be visited upon those who are seeking to oppress and destroy His people. His long forbearance with the wicked emboldens men in transgression, but their punishment is nonetheless certain and terrible because it is long delayed .... The plagues upon Egypt when God was about to deliver Israel were similar in character to those more terrible and extensive judgments which are to fall upon the world just before the final deliverance of God's people. (*The Great Controversy*, pp. 627, 628)

Taking a closer look at Moses, we notice his trust in God growing stronger with the passing of each plague. Remember when God first called him to return to Egypt to free His people Moses was terrified? "*NO!*" was his reaction. "Not me, Lord!"

Forty years is a long time in anyone's life, but eighty years—that is more than most people live. And for one to change his entire way of thinking, his complete way of living—who could do such a thing? Remember Moses was married, settled down and had a family. His life was completely different from what he grew up with.

In the desert he saw his sons grow toward manhood. His family life was well established and just imagine being eighty and hearing God say, "It is time! You are now ready for what I want you to do."

Is it any wonder he had questions? His lifestyle was one of solitude. Think about it. Live for eighty years then forsake everything. Why? Moses was timid, alone much of the time and satisfied. He had put Egypt behind him as if it never happened. The person he was had disappeared. But now God told him to go back and do a work in Egypt. No wonder he had questions. Wouldn't you? Every atom in his body rebelled and cried out, "NO! I want to be invisible."

Although he had changed, Moses was still the same man. Yes, he was older, but he was the same Moses who left Egypt except for one thing, his inner self had become one with God. He bowed low before his Maker and humbly said, "Yes, Lord, I don't understand it and I don't need to know, but I will do as You ask. I will go."

God must have smiled as He pointed the way.

Moses was not the runaway prince of Egypt any longer. He was a self-assured egotist then, but not now. During the seventh plague, the plague of hail, we notice a change.

> Beginning with the seventh plague Moses steps forward as the sole agent of God.
>
> When calling the representatives of the Israelites, Pharaoh still sent for both Moses and Aaron as the two with whom he had been dealing from the time the plagues began. But Moses had now become God's spokesman in the presence of the king, and executor of the divine judgments. By now he must have lost his timidity and fearfulness and become the dauntless champion for the cause of God that he remained till the close of his life. (*The SDA Bible Commentary*, vol. 1, p. 539)

This is not unusual when one steps away from self to rely on God entirely. This kind of action allows the world to see God's leading influence, love, and care. Moses was such an individual. He was a combination of a prince and a shepherd, a new man.

On that fateful night of plague number ten, there were two strong forces working against each other. Moses was involved and blamed for this plague and every other event thus far. In Exodus 12:11, 12 we find it was the Lord Himself who would inflict the tenth and final plague. Verse 12 definitely states that "I will pass through the land ... and will smite all the firstborn ...."

A lot was at stake here. The Israelites and the Egyptians were not the only ones watching this conflict. Heaven, angels, and unfallen worlds were observing each move. All had witnessed what Lucifer said and did in heaven. He implied that God was a tyrant, a dictator and anyone who believed Him was nothing but God's captive slave.

Although loyal to God, some heavenly beings had lingering questions that were yet to be answered. Lucifer was clever and he possessed superior intellect. Unfallen, sinless beings had adored him, but now he was kicked out of heaven, never to return. There was no question that he had been wrong, because he was, but God did not destroy him. He let him live. Why? This still lingered in the minds of many unfallen beings.

So now we have a situation, a nation of slaves and a stubborn dictator controlling their every move and God's appointed spokesman fighting for and with Him in an ongoing war, a deadly conflict. The outcome is not the question here, instead it is how God will accomplish a victory through Moses. This is what many were waiting for. How would He do it? This, in itself, once and for all time, would silence those with lingering questions and perplexing thoughts.

The complete answer would come, not in the time of Moses, but thousands of years later in a man named Jesus.

11

Night the Angel Came

Sunset spread a jewel-like picture above the desert. The sky looked as if it was on fire. Blankets of blue burst into brilliant yellow and pink. Swirling together they merged into dazzling shades of transparent orange, and far below, earths distant horizons became one as a great round disk, a ball of flame glowed soft and dim as it slowly sank in a sea of lavender mist. Darkness, with greedy fingers of purple and blue, began its show of power as it inched forward, covering the low hills of ancient Egypt.

Now far overhead, shining and shimmering in all their glory, blinked tiny beads of brilliant lights. Night, in all its glory, had arrived. That night was like all others except for one thing. An angel was moving among the stars.

And what about Egypt? It sat silent and content. Its capital city felt no danger except for a few nervous officials. These wondered about what Moses had said to Pharaoh. His past warnings all came true and now they felt fear. Was this night different from all others?

Children had been put to bed early. Adults did the same, yet a fire burned here and there, for not all were sleeping. The flames offered light, warmth and a sense of security. Then they too burned low and went cold. The only sound that followed was the occasional barking of a dog or a crying baby.

The section called Goshen was the same except for one difference. The people, the Israelites were packed and ready to move at a moment's notice. Most were not sure where they would be going, but go it was and they were ready to travel. The Israelites and some of the Egyptians were expecting something to happen.

Hours passed slower than usual as they waited. The Israelites were not idle. They were praying in small and large groups. Some were reviewing what had happened during the past number of months and now God was about to rescue them from slavery and they knew it. But waiting was not easy, yet wait they did.

About midnight a small light appeared. It was moving in one of the Egyptian homes. A mother was checking on her newborn child. It was her first.

Suddenly a high-pitched, ear-piercing scream filled the air. It was not a cry of pain or injury. It came with deep terror. People came running. This was followed by another blood-curdling scream, then another and still another. And they were not only coming from that first home. Crying and screaming and shouting erupted in every part of the city and out in the countryside as well until it seemed the entire nation had become one continuous, heart-rending, screeching yell. It went on and on. Old, young, boys, girls, men, women, even animals were dead. No home was without one or more who had died. No home, that is, where the blood was not put on the doorposts. From palaces to homeless people the cry was the same. There was no stopping it. Those uninterrupted shrieks, cries and shouts became like thunder rising from blasts of powerful, devastating storms. Pharaoh himself was not exempt. His son and heir was dead. The angel of death had passed among them.

Goshen and the Israelite nation had not been touched by this plague. God and the appearance of the lamb's blood on their doorposts had saved them. Exodus 12:31 tells what happened next. "And he [Pharaoh] called for Moses and Aaron by night, and said, Rise up, and get you forth from among my people, both ye and the children of Israel; and go, serve the LORD, as ye have said." Verse 32 states that Pharaoh had at last acknowledged the true God. It reads in part as he said, "... be gone; and bless me also."

We know the feelings of the Egyptian people also. They had had enough. "And the Egyptians were urgent upon the people [the slave nation], that they might send them out of the land in haste; for they said, We be all dead men" (Exod. 12:33). The Egyptians, including Pharaoh, were glad to see the Hebrew people leave. In fact, as pointed out, they were more than happy to help them on their way.

And the miracles of God never stopped when the Israelites left Egypt. They continued stronger than ever. Evidence for this comes from the fact that a great cloud was leading them (the Hebrew nation) on their route (Exod. 13:21). This cloud assured the Israelites that God not only knew the way, but that He was present with every step they took. That same cloud was with them day and night. It had a dual purpose. The cloud appeared as fire at night. This gave light and heat for the camp. Then during the day, the cloud provided shade. This was God's assurance that He never left them, day or night.

This movement has come to be known through the ages as the Exodus. Those men, women, boys, girls, flocks and herds were not only leaving Egypt to worship God in the wilderness, they were leaving Egypt forever. They were following God wherever He led, for all times.

The SDA Bible Commentary, vol. 1, page 563, states:

> The fact that the pillar of cloud remained with Israel throughout their long journey, even when they were unfaithful, is assurance to the Christian that God will not soon forsake him on his way through life .... There is no experience of life in which God withdraws Himself. He is present in the darkest nights of misery and disappointment as well as on the brightest days of gladness and success .... The visible pillar is no longer to be seen, but God's presence can still be felt .... Blessed is the man whose eyes are not dim but that he can discern the leading of the Lord.

Satan lost his battle in Egypt and was in a rage because of it. He tried to destroy the Israelites by keeping them in slavery. But the main reason for their rescue was that they were the people of God who chose to reveal to others and the world who the true God was. They were also the only people who were aware of the purpose of Satan's deranged mind who was losing the battle against God. Thus, in his twisted mind he was determined to somehow stop or destroy these people at any cost. He would fight on anyway. He would weaken their influence.

As a last attempt to stop them, he turned again to the power-thirsty monarch of Egypt, Pharaoh. He planted in the mind of this king the thought that he had acted foolishly by allowing the slaves to leave. Exodus 14:5 tells us that Pharaoh and his servants [officials] were upset with themselves for allowing the Israelites to leave. Their entire workforce was gone. Here again we have Satan showing himself through them.

Pharaoh gathered an army of his best, elite armed forces, 600 chariots (with two men in each chariot, one being an armed warrior), plus, "… his horsemen [troops on horseback], and his army" (Exod. 14:9). They would go after them. It may be that many of the troops were from Pharaoh's special and personal bodyguard.

One day's travel would take them completely out of Egypt and from the reach of Pharaoh. But the Lord had other plans. He changed their course to the southwest. This did not make sense, but if God said to go southwest, then southwest it would be. This change put them in a serious situation. As we know from Bible record, they soon faced the Red Sea with no way to cross it. They were at a standstill. This gave Pharaoh's army time to catch up with them. So, from all appearances, the Israelites found themselves trapped with no way of escape.

To the east was the Red Sea. On the south was a rough mountain area with jagged surfaces. Desert stretched to the west with its rugged mountains and to the north came Pharaoh's army. They were doomed.

This was God's doing, but people shouted bitterly at Moses instead. They knew for sure they were going to die. This is usually a normal human reaction. We tend to blame someone else for bad things that happen.

And Moses was their target. They accused him that he should have known better. He and they had followed the cloud and it led to a trap. In reality they were blaming God for their hopeless situation.

Two things were happening. God deliberately placed His people in a hopeless, deadly situation. He was actually testing their faith. Hardships and harsh trials lay ahead and they needed to know that God was always with them, protecting them no matter what the situation was. God was also demonstrating to the Egyptian nation that He was the only God and that their senseless idols were nothing but just that: useless trash.

Again, we now notice another change in Moses. He is not the same man in spirit and action. The timid person he was when he first approached Pharaoh is now gone.

In spite of this he seemed somewhat discouraged. Things were going well; he and God were close friends. But there was something that bothered him. It was not because of Pharaoh and his hard headedness. No, it was because of Israel's lack of faith in God. He expected more from them.

With what they had been through, seen and heard in Egypt, the powerful plagues, their protection, the cloud and their escape, God's presence with them, all of this and more, they still whined and complained. Egypt was still in them. Is it any wonder that Moses was disappointed and downhearted?

As a result, he quietly and calmly faced these hard to handle people trying to assure them that all would be well. He knew the people were scared as they faced the unknown and that there was no turning back and he had no idea how God would handle His people, but he knew He would do it somehow.

The plagues of Egypt had not only taught the Egyptians just who God was, they also strengthened Moses to rely entirely and completely on Him. His faith was secure in God and God alone. That would never change.

His words to those scared, hot-headed, faithless Israelites were recorded in Exodus 14:13, 14, "And Moses said unto the people, Fear ye not, stand still, and see the salvation of the LORD, which He will shew to you to day: for the Egyptians whom ye have seen to day, ye shall see them again no more forever. The Lord shall fight for you, and ye shall hold your peace." The words "hold your peace" explain everything. Should we do less in our time of uncertainty, distress, hardship, and trial?

God, who was in the cloud, placed Himself between His people and Pharaoh's army. It stopped them cold. That protective cloud became a wall of darkness to Pharaoh and his men. They could not go through it, but on Israel's side that same cloud was shade during the day and a fiery torch at night. Thus, they faced the Red Sea.

And, what were the Israelites supposed to do? They were not to stand by and do nothing while God rescued them. He had plans for them.

They were scared, of course. Pharaoh and his grand army were there ready, armed, and eager to destroy each and every one of them. The Hebrews complained loud and long about it to Moses. They blamed him and Aaron for everything.

God, who was in the cloud, placed Himself between His people and Pharaoh's army. It stopped them cold. That protective cloud became a wall of darkness to Pharaoh and his men. They could not go through it, but on Israel's side that same cloud was shade during the day and a fiery torch at night.

But the cloud kept both sides in check. Neither side moved. This was a time of waiting, a time for each person on both sides of the cloud to search their inner being for a reason why they chose who to trust and believe in. The delay was nerve-shattering. And that waiting stretched on and on with seemingly no end in sight.

But then these words of Moses rang in their ears, "[S]tand still, and see the salvation of the LORD" (Exod. 14:13). This was followed by an order. "Forward! Move forward to the sea!" That was the action they were asked to do. "Don't just stand there. Move! Move forward to the Red Sea and get your feet wet!"

Complaining and not understanding, they followed orders blindly and dazed. They moved. They obeyed. They went to the water's edge and stepped into it.

Moses, rod in hand, stretched it toward the water and a dry path, a road, opened before their startled eyes. They couldn't believe what they saw. It led across the sea floor clear to the other side.

But take note, it didn't happen until they got their feet wet, then and only then. Off they ran, running as fast as they could go, shouting all the way. Walls of water stood on end and churned on both sides of them. They raced across dry ground to the far side of the sea and safety. Ellen White states, "The people were weary and terrified, yet if they had held back when Moses bade them advance, God would never have opened the path for them" (*Patriarchs and Prophets*, p. 290).

But what about the Egyptian army and Pharaoh? The cloud that held them back had lifted and when Pharaoh saw what had happened, he stared in disbelief. He was speechless. Then Satan took over. He whispered in his ear, "Go after them. The way is still open." Pharaoh hesitated until Satan spoke louder, "GO!" He opened his mouth and yelled, "*FORWARD!*"

No one moved.

His mighty army just stayed in place transfixed, not believing what they were looking at. "GO!" he yelled again. This was followed by threats. The army acted as one man. They took off thundering across that dry land in the sea. Horses pounding, running feet, rolling wheels, and rattling chariots all raced together. The noise rose to a high pitch. Orders were to go after the Israelites and destroy each and every one of them. They obeyed and were instantly in action and sped on their way.

The Israelites, safe on the other side, saw them coming and they began to panic when suddenly a roll of ear-piercing thunder sounded. Next, the sky opened with howling, screaming wind followed by great crashes of lightning and more thunder. The walls of water holding back the sea came roaring back together again.

The army tried to turn back, but it was too late. They disappeared. Everything, everyone, horses, chariots, equipment, soldiers were destroyed. They had finally felt the power of the God of heaven and earth. They paid the supreme price. They all died. Pharaoh collapsed in floods of tears and unbelief with his captions of authority around him in distress and horror. All that was left of his great army was broken weapons, bits of chariots and the lifeless forms of horses and men drifting on water as they slowly washed ashore.

Did the Israelites learn the lessons of faith? Have we?

12

They Sang and Danced

They were now on the opposite shore of the Red Sea. Safe on dry land—every one of them. Families, possessions, animals, everything was intact. Best of all, their enemies were gone. There was no more threat.

Thousands of voices burst into praises with shouting, singing, and dancing. Their cries of joy and relief could be heard for miles. Even the complainers joined in.

> Like the voice of the great deep, rose from the vast hosts of Israel that sublime ascription [praise]. It was taken up by the women of Israel, Miriam, the sister of Moses, leading the way, as they went forth with timbrel [tambourine and/or a hand drum] and dance. Far over desert and sea rang the joyous refrain, and the mountains re-echoed the words of their praise—"Sing ye to Jehovah, for He hath triumphed gloriously." (*Patriarchs and Prophets*, pp. 288, 289)

Modern, or social dancing, should not be compared with the religious dance of Bible times. Men and women were never physical or embracing one another in this function. They were separated at all times. This was the dancer's way of expressing love, devotion, and thanksgiving to God. And God approved.

There is a Scripture that all Christians should pay attention to. It's found in Deuteronomy. The words were spoken directly to Moses from God. God led the Israelites from the center of a large cloud. This verse, however, brings God much closer than it did when He spoke through that cloud. It was not only spoken to the Hebrews, but also to you who read it.

Here is that verse. The Revised Standard Version reads, "Because the LORD your God walks in the midst of your camp, to save you and to give up your enemies before you, therefore your camp [lifestyle] must be holy, that he may not see anything indecent among you, and turn away from you" (Deut. 23:14, RSV).

It reminds one of the times when He walked with Adam and Eve every day in Eden. This applies to everything we do and own, the way we dress, what we eat, drink, think, act and say. These were and still are clear rules. Nothing is overlooked.

In today's fast paced, crime and drug world it means hard work for every Christian believer, man, woman, and child.

The cosmos around us is a prime example of this. The universe is orderly. Each heavenly body functions and operates exactly as it is expected to. Laws and regulations hold fixed stars and their galaxies in place. They function together and are never out of place. Each has its individual purpose, unchanging and obeying all the rules. All operate together with perfect order and precision.

Even waste in outer space functions by strict rules. Asteroids and meteorites are all accounted for. If they were not, the earth itself would be a target for hits, leaving pockmarks like those on the surface of the moon. If one or more of these flying objects should hit the earth, we might all disappear. God guides and places these flying missiles exactly where He wants them.

God told Moses that the Israelite camp was to be clean and orderly and He meant just that. Otherwise He would not walk among them as they mingled with each other. Thus, instead of being hidden in that cloud above them, He longed to be among them.

God is doing the same thing right now, just as He did then. He is, if you let Him, in every room of your house. What does He see and hear?

Looking at Moses physically was just like looking at any other human male figure. He walked, talked, ate, laughed, cried, loved, and functioned as all of us do. Yet there was something about this man that set him apart from others. Moses was different. For there, in the desert, on the other side of the Red Sea, God had him standing as the leader of His chosen people. Why was this? What made him different from other people?

This man was born at a time when ruthless people controlled the lives and destiny of millions of others. He was a male child from a family of slaves destined to die even before his birth. Instead, he was suddenly thrust from an appointment with death to live in the coveted halls of the most powerful king in all the earth, the Pharaoh of Egypt. Once there, he was treated and respected, not only as a royal and loved prince of the realm, but as heir apparent to the throne itself.

What a story!

Yet in his future, as the story goes, in a moment of rage, Moses lost it all. That part of his life will be told later, but for now we see God molding this man's thinking and behavior. This not only reveals the leading of God in a person's life, but also a detailed training period.

And Moses was willing. That makes all the difference. What did the future hold for this human being? We shall soon find out. God had plans. He chose him to represent Him to a fallen world.

13

Shur

The cloud moved. It slowly advanced to the southeast. This sign meant it was time to move on. Camp was broken up and they followed its leading. The path led along the shore of the sea and on into the hostile desert of Shur. This vast area touched Egypt's eastern border. Next, the cloud turned north, then finally to the southern border of Palestine. To the far south stretched the mountains of the Sinai Peninsula.

If this route were followed today, one would come across the oasis of Marah. Its location is approximately forty-seven miles from Suez. Exodus 15:23 states its water is bitter and not drinkable. The Bible names this place Marah. Thus, we have thousands of thirsty people with nothing to drink. Water gushed before them, but it was worthless.

Three days before this, these people were singing and dancing for joy. Their enemies lay dead. They were free at last knowing that God's promise of a new home, a land overflowing with milk and honey would soon be theirs. But now this—and no water to drink! What was God doing to them now?

Hordes of frustrated, maddened humanity exploded in the face of Moses. As always, he was the one to blame. They shouted that he led them there to die. Yelling, shaking fists and with twisted, distorted faces they threatened his life.

Moses called to God in prayer. He needed help and he needed it now. God came to his rescue by telling him what to do to sweeten the water to a drinkable state. "… [T]he LORD showed him a tree. When he had thrown *it* into the waters, the waters were made sweet" (Exod. 15:25, MEV).

> The great lesson here taught is for all time. Often the Christian life is beset by dangers, and duty seems hard to perform. The imagination pictures impending ruin before and bondage or death behind. Yet the voice of God speaks clearly, "Go forward." We should obey this command, even though our eyes cannot penetrate the darkness, and we feel the cold waves about our feet. (Ibid., p. 290)

So what was it that God was doing to His people? The answer comes from *The SDA Bible Commentary*, vol. 1, page 574. "From the time of their departure from Egypt to their entry onto Canaan, God 'proved' [tested] His people on many occasions, first at the Red Sea, now at Marah … and elsewhere. These 'proofs' [trials] were part of God's attempts to train them, under comparatively easy circumstances, for the experiences they would face in Canaan."

What does our future Canaan, yours and mine, look like? Shall we expect different treatment as we prepare for it? The answer is no. Refining comes first. "The path where God leads the way may lie through the desert or the sea, but it is a safe path" (*Patriarchs and Prophets*, p. 290).

Later, at the oasis of Elim, it was a different story. When they reached this place the cry went up, "*Water!*" There was plenty of good, fresh, drinkable water. There were trees too. Like children at play they stayed three days. Then the cloud moved on just as they began running out of food.

God's trials were in effect again and, oh how they complained. Only this time it was not just the regular families; it was sheepherders and cattlemen who joined in as well. They were creating a rebellious uproar. Israelite leaders and even the elders joined the cry.

Once again, as always, they blamed Moses. They also pointed fingers of blame at Aaron. *"FOOD,"* was the demand *"WE WANT FOOD!"* The whole nation grumbled loud and strong against Moses and Aaron in the wilderness. "Would to God," they said, "we had died by the hand of the LORD in the land of Egypt, when we sat by the flesh pots, and when we did eat bread to the full; for ye have brought us forth into this wilderness, to kill this whole assembly with hunger" (Exod. 16:3).

They dared to and, even worse yet, were bold enough to say these things after all the miracles they had seen. What kind of human beings were these people anyway? When the going got rough, all they could think about was themselves. Does that sound familiar?

Yet, God saw great good in these people. His love and care for each and every one of them ran deep, strong and lasting. And what was the reaction of Moses? Did he shout back, rant or rage as he did years before when he killed the Egyptian? That was a common action for him when he was in authority as a prince. But time and being alone with God for forty years in the wilds produced a changed and subdued man. He was not the same person.

He knew these people had food. That was not the real issue. They were thinking of the future, of the tomorrows to come. They were living in a fiercely dry desert where no one dared go—except them. There was no place to store or preserve their basic needs such as food and water. Faith was still an unknown factor.

Moses saw their misery and self-inflicted suffering. What was his reaction? A strong feeling of sorrow filled him. But this, and his quiet manner, made them more irritated. Didn't he care?

In an article from *The Signs of the Times* magazine dated April 8, 1880, Ellen White described what happened next. In my own words this is what she wrote.

While this uproar was going on, a change in the cloud's appearance began to take place. Sounds of muffled thunder grew deep and loud. Lights flashed and rolled within that great pillar; even the color began changing.

Suddenly a voice sounded. It was like none other ever heard. It exploded in their ears petrifying them with fear. This was the voice of God.

He had heard their complaining, fault finding, and blame accusing Him and Moses for all their trouble. He called Moses and Aaron to approach the cloud. This had always been forbidden. But now God ordered them to come and when they did, He repeated to them, as He had stated before to Moses, that He would send abundant meat and bread to them at evening and again in the morning. He also told them that He knew the Israelites complaints were actually against Him, not His chosen leaders.

"God did not show Himself offended at their murmuring but sent help each time they were in trouble. In so doing it was His purpose to train them to trust their divinely appointed leaders and to have faith in Him" (*The SDA Bible Commentary*, vol. 1, p. 577).

Ever since Adam and Eve, God has had a problem with the human race. Before the fall, God talked with people face to face. But that all changed. This being the case, prayer, the written Word, and belief in who God is became man's means of communication with Him.

God understood the Israelites better than they did themselves. He was well aware that their faith and trust in Him was weak. So basically, they didn't know Him. Therefore, faith in Him was primitive and undeveloped just as it was when they lived in Egypt. As a result, there was little change in their conception of Him as they traveled behind the cloud in the deserts of northern Africa.

He had a dual purpose for hiding His presence in that cloud. First, He wanted them to have physical evidence without actually seeing Him directly. This made Him one with them. Second, He could communicate from inside the cloud with Moses on their behalf. Through this means He wanted them to realize that He was well aware of their needs and would provide what they asked Him for. But His presence scared them because He knew at all times everything they said and did.

Although there is no cloud to see and guide us today, God's patience and understanding is no different. He still guides each one of us on earth, that is if we allow Him to do so. Patience, care, and understanding are miracles from God Himself.

Since God had promised meat to eat, which they really wanted, quail, by the thousands, swarmed over the desert that evening. It being a familiar table bird, the tents of the encampment were filled with meat. People ate it until they could eat no more. They were more than satisfied.

Quail is a migratory bird ranging through Europe, Asia, and Africa. They are also found in the United States. It is not a large bird, approximately ten inches in length. They feed mainly on seed. They breed on the ground laying from nine to fifteen yellowish, brown spotted eggs. In Africa, C. Delegorguei as they are called, are numbered in the hundreds of thousands, if not more.

> *Although there is no cloud to see and guide us today, God's patience and understanding is no different. He still guides each one of us on earth, that is if we allow Him to do so. Patience, care, and understanding are miracles from God Himself.*

But quail was not all that God sent. He also promised bread. The following morning, after the dew evaporated, a soft white substance was left behind. It was something the people had never seen before. And when tasted, it melted sweetly in their mouth. Moses called it manna; it was God's bread sent from heaven.

From then on, wherever they traveled, this manna appeared every morning. It was not to be kept overnight because it would spoil. This morning experience was a reminder for them to remember that God was faithfully caring for their daily needs. God has not changed. He still provides for our daily needs. As the slave nation of Egypt vanished into the wilderness, He went with them. He never left them, not once.

Closer to our day, there are two current stories involving this same God. Both are true. Both happened during the Vietnam War in the

Far East. These demonstrate the tender care of God for His people in times of great danger and in deep distress.

A Christian family was trapped in their home in the city of Saigon as enemy soldiers closed in. There was a mother, father and two small children. News reached them somehow that the airport was still open and people were escaping by air. But the question was, how could they possibly get to the airport? Martial Law was in effect. Streets were blocked and patrolled by armed soldiers with orders to shoot and kill anyone on the streets, no matter who they were.

This family knelt and talked with God. They told Him of their situation which He already knew. Following prayer, they gathered a few belongings, opened the door of their home, and stepped onto the street. The airport was within walking distance. They didn't cling to the sidewalks or slink along the sides of buildings. Instead they walked close together and made their way down the center of the street.

Yes, they saw armed soldiers. They were everywhere, but on they went, up one street then down another. At last, the airport was within sight, and this was the most dangerous area of all. Fighting was happening all around it, but it was still open. Planes were still flying out. They could see them take off. They walked through the fighting, the blockade and on into the airport itself.

They made it and soon were flying to safety. What happened here? God walked beside that family as they nervously made their way to safety. He had made them invisible to everyone and everything around them. He protected and guided them as He did for the Israelites of long ago. He has not changed and He never will.

This family came to the United States and found employment where I worked at the Pacific Press in California, a Seventh-day Adventist Publishing Company.

The second story is similar. It also happened during that same war. A Christian man was captured and put in prison. Before his capture he was on heavy medication. He needed it to live. Now, he had none of it and was steadily growing weaker and weaker. He faithfully prayed about it. Did God hear him?

Near the prison was an area of wealthy homes. These people had some measure of freedom and could move about. A lady friend of the man in confinement, aware of his condition, was impressed to do something about his condition. She knew what he needed. Buying the medication he needed, she had her car brought around with its driver, then they drove to the prison. The car was parked in front of the main entrance to the building. She got out, walked to the main gate, and went inside. Finding her way past desks and armed soldiers she finally stood before the locked door where this man was being held. She reached for the latch, turned it, opened the locked door, and went inside. The man was startled. She handed him the medicine he needed. They talked briefly then she left. Finding her way back to the waiting car, she got in and was driven home. God had shut the eyes of those prison guards when this woman left her parked car, walked past each soldier, and opened a locked door. The man lived and in time was released.

God is still, and always will be, the same loving, caring God as He always has been since time began. Malachi 3:6 says, "For I am the LORD, I change not." He never stops or changes in taking care of those who love, obey, serve, and call on Him. God works the same for you every day, even when you don't know He is doing it.

14

Up in the Air

God had just provided unlimited food for the Israelites. They were happy and said so. Yet with their next breath, they pointed fingers at God and Moses, accusing both for not giving them water to drink. They trusted neither of them. Shouting defiance again and showing anger they roared, "Who is this Moses and why did he bring us to this forsaken place to die? God will kill us all!"

All they had to do was ask for water. God never denied them anything essential, especially water. He would have gladly given it abundantly. These accusations were, in reality, directed at Moses blaming him as the cause of their troubles, in this case the lack of water.

Acting like spoiled children they also blamed God for appointing Moses as their leader. Looking back at their history we ask, "How could they be so ungrateful?" Stupidity and unthankful would be better words.

So, what did God do about the water situation? He gave it to them, lots of it, plus a lesson they would never forget. There is a sentence in *Patriarchs and Prophets*, page 293, that fits this situation. It reads, "Though their present needs are supplied, many are unwilling to trust God for the future."

Although water was supplied, a penalty came with it. Their greatest need was not water. Trust in God was their greatest need, and not only trust, but believing He cared for and watched over every breath they took. The penalty for their rebellious attitude and self-centered unbelief came from the very place where God supplied this water.

It was in Amalekite territory. These people were wild and warlike, constantly raiding the slow-moving Israelites at the rear of that traveling nation. Joshua, at the command of Moses, gathered men from all the tribes to fight these attackers. This meant war and they were outnumbered, but they fought for their lives.

Moses, a trained military man and ex-general, took a position on a hill overlooking the battlefield. He was in full sight of both sides. Two men stood beside him. They were Aaron and Hur. Aaron, we know, was his brother and a priest, but who was Hur? There is very little known about him except he was one of the men close to Moses and he was also a leader in the Exodus. He was also a descendent of Judah through Caleb, and there is some thought that he was either the husband of Miriam, or her son (See *SDA Bible Commentary*, vol. 1, p. 585, note for Exod. 17:10).

The reason for Moses being on the hill was to encourage Joshua and his men in battle. They could see him. But Moses was not just standing or sitting on that hill, his arms were outstretched toward heaven and he was in deep prayer for the successful outcome of the battle.

As long as he was in that position and in an attitude of prayer, the armies of Israel were winning. If, however, his arms lowered or drooped, the Amalekites were winning. Aaron and Hur were there to help, for whenever he began to drop his arms, they would grab them and hold them up. A seat was finally brought for Moses to sit on as the two men continued holding his arms high in the air. This went on for hours. Actually, there were two battles taking place here. One raged on the battlefield while the other was on the hill.

As the night fell, the Israelite men won the war. The Amalekites were defeated, and Moses was exhausted. Besides pleading with God for His people, those arms of his were almost frozen in an upright position such as a statue would be. This demonstrated that "... divine strength is to be combined with human effort" (Ibid., p. 299).

Moses must have been a powerful man. Although he was white-headed and old, he was unusually strong. Physically he was like a machine, a mighty force of energy to endure and overcome any resistance with overwhelming strength. This was a gift granted by God for the benefit and influence of the work he was destined and authorized to do. Remember, he was in his eighties at the battle between Joshua and the Amalekites.

And would you believe when Moses was 120 years old the Bible states he was in the best of health and strength? Deuteronomy 34:7, MEV, states that "Moses was a hundred and twenty years old when he died. His eye was not dim, nor was his vitality diminished."

God and Moses chose each other. Moses knew, loved, and obeyed the one and only true God of heaven and earth. This pleased God so much that they became close friends forever. This is just what the Israelite nation needed, to learn and to trust, instead of complaining about lack of water or any other thing.

Ellen White explains this situation and the background partnership. In part it reads as follows:

> The Amalekites were not ignorant of God's character or of His sovereignty, but instead of fearing before Him, they had set themselves to defy His power. The wonders wrought [produced] by Moses before the Egyptians were made a subject of mockery by the people of Amalek, and the fears of surrounding nations were ridiculed. They had taken oath by their gods that they would destroy the Hebrews ... and they boasted that Israel's God would be powerless to resist them .... [But] The care of God is over the weakest of His children .... Over all who love and fear Him, His hand extends as a shield. (Ibid., p. 300)

Thus, the Amalek people have, to this day, been blotted out of human history and memory forever (see Deut. 25:19).

News of the water miracle, manna, quail, and the victory against the Amalek people spread. Most of the action of these events took place near the area where Jethro, the father-in-law of Moses lived. He knew what was going on. But he was not the only one to receive reports of these happenings. They spread for hundreds of miles in every direction to people, tribes, and nations. Egypt too was well aware of the Israelites and their powerful God. The news went out: leave them alone; don't bother them, for if you do, you will lose. Moses, the Hebrew nomads, and God was a power to fear.

Jethro went to see Moses. He took Zipporah, the wife of Moses, and their sons, Gershom and Eliezer, with him. Moses was completely overjoyed. After all, he was a family man and they happily celebrated the reunion with a feast dedicated to God. Moses excitedly told everything God had done on their long, hard trek through the wilderness. There were miracles, triumphs, and failures. He spoke of loyalty and betrayers, rebellion and faithful followers. But most of all he told of the blessings received and of the careful leading of their loving, protecting God who never left them.

It was on this visit that Jethro, the ever-wise priest of Midian, noticed a problem. He saw how people were using Moses and how it was draining his strength. He watched as day after day Moses sat listening and solving vital, and not so important, problems for all those thousands of people. He was their recognized leader and his decisions were law. Moses alone was the problem-solver for that entire nation and he turned no one away. As a result, he had no time for anything else. Jethro pointed this out to him.

Moses answered, "This gives me a chance to instruct them in the statutes and laws of God. They need faith!" "But," answered Jethro, "They are draining your strength and wearing you out. You can't go on like this." "Jethro," he replied, "It needs to be done and people are looking to me for help." Jethro answered back, "There are other wise, God fearing men in the camp who know the laws and statutes as you do. Select and appoint some of them to preside over the smaller problems while you handle the serious ones. Then, things will run smoother and you will keep up your strength."

Moses saw the wisdom and took his advice. The result was immediate, and things became smoother and far more efficient. This speaks well of Moses. Although he was a powerful leader with authority, it was not beneath him to accept advice. He had listened then accepted the plan from his father-in-law and was happy he did so. It worked. This is the mark of a great person.

But now, the cloud was moving again.

15

Would They Say YES?

Tents were taken down, folded, and tied in place. Tools, cooking pots, dishes, drinking vessels, clothing, children, flocks, herds, and people were all packed up and ready to go. Then, amid the lowing of cattle, the bleating of sheep and goats, they slowly, steadily followed where the cloud led. The cloud too was slow. God knew it took time for relocation. He was patient with their forward march.

Passing high mountain ranges, they crossed hot desert sands and went on into craggy canyon passes. Impossible places for travel opened and they went through. On cold, clear nights, under millions of glittering stars, the cloud turned to fire and kept them warm. That same cloud also shaded them in daylight; shielding them from the relentless, burning heat.

One day, while struggling through a steep gorge, a way suddenly opened and before their eyes stretched a wondrous sight: an open valley. It stretched to the foot of a majestic mountain called Sinai. On the very top, at its crown, rested the cloud of God.

Here, in that valley, they came to a stop and raised their tents for a long stay. God had this place in mind when He began His leading from their bondage. In this place they could be isolated from outside influences. There they would live with Him for almost a year and be taught by the God of the universe. And, when the time was right, they would spread His divine message across the earth that God is real, that He is love.

What did the place look like?

Eyewitness accounts tell us that it was a flat, brush-filled desert of nearly two miles in length and one-half mile wide. Mountains surrounded it, forming an oval shape below the lofty peak. A few of the Israelites, it is thought, may have chosen adjacent valleys, southeast and west, to pitch their tents. Even there Mount Sinai dominated the scene.

To the southeast was a cliff of granite. It soared straight up, creating an appearance of a high altar. From there God's voice could be heard. Below it was slightly raised knolls or earth embankments acting as barriers to keep people from touching the mountain itself. Exodus 19:12, MEV, states that "Whoever touches the mountain will surely be put to death." Moses knew this place well, for it was here where he saw the burning bush.

The journey to this place had been a hectic, sometimes hair-raising trip. Many of the travelers were exhausted and confused. But now they found a place of safety separated from others, and a resting place to reflect upon who they were and what God wanted from and for them. They were alone with their God.

Mark 6:31, 32 applied to them as it did centuries later to the disciples of Jesus when He said, "… Come ye yourselves apart into a desert place, and rest a while …. And they departed into a desert place …." Periods of rest, peace and quiet are vital for all people to be alone with God.

No sooner was Moses able to settle himself, rest and catch his breath when he heard God calling him to climb the mountain. Thousands watched as Moses climbed the mountain. It was easy at first then harder as he struggled higher and higher. He also knew all Israel was wondering what was next, and he was right for far below eyes followed his every move until they couldn't see him anymore.

They stayed way back from the base of the mountain because of God's warning not to go near or touch it. Most of the time the summit was hidden from view, clouds completely covered it. There were rumbling sounds coming from deep within its massive structure. They sounded like thunder. Strange flashes and light streaked across the face of rocky cliffs and at times ran down to the ground, shaking the earth. At times the tiny far-off figure of Moses was spotted. He was almost at the top. Many watchers were on their knees praying. A few were in tears.

Suddenly Moses was gone. He had vanished and only the cloud remained. Some wondered if they would ever see him again.

But in time Moses did come back, and when he did, he had many, many things to tell them. He and God had talked about many things and when they were finished, he brought back new laws, rules, and obligations to present to the nation.

Through all of this, God was giving an expression of His affection, friendship, and respect through His set of regulations for the Hebrew people to accept and live by. He was asking for them to accept His offer or reject it and Him. The choice was theirs. Was it a yes or a no?

God, the Lord of the universe was asking them to be His. The full power of this offer came centuries later by the greatest Gift God could and would ever give by offering His Son, His only Son, on the cross of Calvary for their salvation.

Moses called the elders together before he said anything to the people about all of this. Would they accept it? The details were not revealed completely. That would come later. Before the masses knew any of the terms and what they meant, each of the leading men answered, "Yes." They accepted God, His laws and way of life.

Now the question was, what will a nation of ex-slaves say? There were rebels among them.

16

Forty Days

Work loomed ahead—hard work—yet, to the relief of Moses, God was in control. After meeting with tribal leaders and priests, Moses and they realized it had to be God Himself who must inform the people of His requirements to be His chosen people. But were the people ready for this? They were not sure.

The way of life for these people had revolved around a ruthless dictator. If they performed well for their Egyptian masters, there were rewards. They also knew that whatever the cost of a rebellious attitude, their overlords would be hard and ruthless. Strong action, often cruelty followed those who did not conform; thus, most Israelites were looking at God as an overseer. They were afraid of Him.

God accepted the leaders' request to have Him come off the mountain and talk directly to the people; however, the camp, the entire nation, was to wash their clothes, their children and themselves first. Tents were to be completely clean. Nothing was to be sloppy or out of place. Cleanliness and order were top priority. Only then would God agree to appear personally and deliver His requirements for obeying Him. This was serious business.

When informed of this, the reaction was one of alarm. There was fear. These people had seen the results of God's actions before. What would He do this time?

Every man, woman and child made ready for God's visit. Everything was a beehive of activity. They were told that God would be there in three days. Exodus 19:11 says, "And be ready against [by] the third day: for the third day the LORD will come down in the sight of all the people upon mount Sinai."

It was quiet the second night except for what was necessary, and after they did their chores they stayed in the safety of their tents. Children were put to bed and told to be quiet. Tents were spotlessly clean both inside and out. Clothes and cooking utensils were sparkling, and everything was in its proper place.

For some, that night was a sleepless one. Yet, there were those who went to bed as if nothing was about to happen. Even they had a hard time sleeping but would never admit it.

Day three dawned amid heavy rumbling from the mountain. Suddenly a blast from a trumpet split the air. People looked at the mountain, the cloud that was always there loomed larger than ever and it was growing. It appeared black. Lightning with long, jagged sheets of flames shot skyward. It appeared as if the entire mountain was on fire. More trumpet blasts came. They were close together and powerful. Following this the cloud grew at a faster rate of speed and size. In a few minutes the entire mountain was hidden. No one dared to look at it, but they did. Moses called for a fence as a barrier around the base, for if any child, person or even an animal wandered close, it would be instant death (*Patriarchs and Prophets*, p. 304. Adapted to writer's view of how things most likely occurred).

People gathered in small and large groups. Most shook with violent reaction, not because they were cold, no, they were completely terrified. God was on His way. Shadows and unclear figures were seen moving inside the cloud. Who or what were they? No one knew. Not one word or even a whisper came from that vast, watching multitude. Finally, a powerful, long trumpet blast sounded. Mothers held children close, others covered their ears. Men stared; women hid their faces.

Then, complete silence.

Not one sound or movement was heard or seen. It was nerve-shattering. Then it came. The clear, strong, deep rolling voice of God. It echoed and re-echoed like crashing thunder racing through canyons, ringing, bouncing back from their jagged, unadorned walls. Flashes of light exploded with ear-piercing thunderbolts. It was awesome, terrible, violent, and startling all at the same time. This continuous sound came directly from one uninterrupted, unquestionable Source, the voice of God Himself.

He was speaking His law, known to us today as the Ten Commandments. Terrified, the Israelites began running in mass panic away from His presence, the sign and sounds of God. They pushed, shoved, trampled on each other and children. They screamed. Where and how could they find a place to hide? There was no place to run from God.

Moses tried stopping the masses, but he had no success. He and God had spoken together before, also in front of the people in times past, but never like this. Shaking from fright, and petrified with fear, they screamed at Moses, their voices nervous and weak at first. But as they continued to shout it grew in strength. Finally, they roared as one voice, "All that the LORD hath spoken we will do" (Exod. 19:8). They had no idea what they were saying. They just accepted blindly what God put before them without understanding any of His rules or laws. They were not prepared for this powerful, terrifying display of glory.

In *Patriarchs and Prophets* we read "The minds of the people, blinded and debased by slavery and heathenism, were not prepared to appreciate fully the far-reaching principles of God's ten precepts. That the obligations of the Decalogue might be more fully understood and enforced, additional precepts were given, illustrating and applying the principles of the Ten Commandments" (p. 310).

And from *The SDA Bible Commentary*, vol. 1, page 595 (note for Exod. 19:8), we find, "The spontaneous cry, 'All that the Lord hath spoken we will do' was without question a superficial demonstration of religious enthusiasm, a momentary reaction to a glorious and sublime truth. There was lacking the spirit of deep, true conversion, the "heart' to do what God demanded' (Deut. 5:29). It is small wonder the people soon apostatized, and worshiped the golden calf."

After this and every time Moses went up on the mountain, he came back and began recording the information and laws God told him to write. His early training in Egypt paid off. Moses knew how to write and his written words filled several books.

Later, and without hesitation, when God called, Moses walked up the mountain. Sometimes he took Aaron or Joshua with him. There were others also at times by God's invitation only. And the masses of people below the mountain became accustomed to this.

But there was one time when they became anxious and questioned. It was because Moses was gone too long and they wondered if something had gone wrong. God had called him up the mountain, and Joshua was to come with him. But as they were about to reach the top, Joshua was left behind while Moses went higher where he was taken into the cloud. This was not unusual except for one thing. Both men were gone for forty days and no one knew what happened to them.

How was it possible for Moses to survive all that time? Exodus 34:28 states, "And he [speaking of Moses] was there with the Lord forty days and forty nights; he did neither eat bread, nor drink water."

The SDA Bible Commentary, vol. 1, page 676, has this comment: "Moses' audience with the Lord sustained his physical strength, and this made food and drink unnecessary. The needs of the body were not felt because the desires of the spirit were so fully met." I assume the same was the case with Joshua.

As days and weeks continued to pass, serious questions came up from the people below. "Where are they? Why are they gone so long?" Some even asked, "Are they dead?"

Remember it was these same people who asked Moses to speak with God personally for them. They did not want to hear the sound of His voice again. It scared them when they heard Him speak and most of the Israelite nation ran away from it. That is why Moses was on the mountain now.

He was their spokesman and only means of communication with God. They wanted it to be that way.

But now tension and doubt crept into the minds of thousands. And without the visible presence of their main leader they began to murmur and complain. Word spread, especially among the former Egyptians and aliens. They had worshiped idols they could see and touch. Now, all they could see from below the mountain was that cloud and nothing was happening.

What was going on? Did God move away leaving the two men behind? Also, many began asking questions like this. "Why did we ever leave Egypt, and did this man Moses bring us here to die? We need a God we can see. This is no good! We want a new god to lead us!"

Aaron was in charge while Moses was absent, so naturally the complainers turned to him for answers. He had none.

A rebellion set in. Sides were taken. Those loyal to God and Moses stood against those who were not. Both held their ground as physical clashes erupted. Things were so out of control that a few of God's loyal followers lost their lives (*Patriarchs and Prophets*, p. 316).

And what was Aaron's position in all this? He tried to negotiate to please both sides. But it was impossible and he knew it. An idol, a god of gold, was demanded.

After witnessing the death of some of God's loyal followers, Aaron was fearful for his own safety. He felt he had to appease those against God's leading. God, it appeared, was not first in his life. Under severe pressure he asked people to give him their golden earrings. He hoped they would not, but they did it gladly. Now what? Did he give in entirely to their demands?

"Here is the gold!" they shouted, "Make us a god!" "Tomorrow!" he promised, "We will worship God." Notice, he didn't say which god. Trying to please both sides he quietly planned a worship service for the real God and at the same time place a calf of gold made from their jewelry to appease the opposition.

Planned deception through disguise is sin. Those people had heard the following words as God spoke them Himself, "Thou shalt [shall] have no other gods before me" (Exod. 20:3). Now here we have a trusted leader of God's people, Aaron, the brother of Moses, deliberately causing and encouraging blasphemers to continue in sin, as Ellen White stated, by replacing Him (God) with an ox (*Patriarchs and Prophets*, p. 317).

And high on Mount Sinai, as God and Moses talked together, a growing rumble could be heard, and it was not coming from the mountain. It rolled upward from below growing stronger and louder. It was from the camp far below. God told Moses to go back down. His people were in a revolt. In Exodus 32:7 we find God's actual words. They read: "And the LORD said unto Moses, Go, get thee down; for thy people, which thou broughtest out of the land of Egypt, have corrupted themselves."

Notice what God was saying. He referred to the Israelites as Moses' people, not His people. He also pointed to them as the ones he, Moses, brought out of Egypt by saying "thou broughtest out of the land of Egypt." In other words, God said the Israelites were not His people. They belonged to Moses alone, for he was the one responsible for them and their current actions. God was in reality saying that He, God, was disowning them.

He also told Moses to "[L]et Me alone" (Exod. 32:10). Those three words "Let Me alone" speak volumes. They tell us that Moses was pleading to save the Israelites. God did tell him He would destroy them and start over with Moses and create a new nation of people through him, but Moses begged, "NO! Don't do that."

Verse 11 tells us much more. It reveals the intelligence and loyalty of this man to both God and God's people. He picked up on the word "thy" and reversed it to "Thy," meaning that these people were not his people, but God's own elect. He said to God that they were His people, the ones that He alone led out of Egypt.

Moses pled with God not to destroy them. After all they had been through and the miracles they had seen to preserve them as His people—to reject them now would mean a defeat for God. This would disgrace God's name and power. The heathen world would rejoice at His failure.

Another argument Moses gave God was this: if You wipe out the Israelites, Egypt and other nations who are watching, will say that God's only purpose was not for them to leave Egypt to worship and sacrifice to Him, but instead to kill them off by sacrificing them. This would dishonor Jehovah and they would say, "I told you so, God is a tyrant not to be trusted. He is not the loving God He claims to be."

Moses was not thinking of himself with these words, he was fighting for the preservation of the Israelites, and God's great name as well.

Actually, God was testing Moses on that mountain top, and Moses came through with flying colors. God was not planning to destroy the Israelites. And the arguments with Moses proved to Him that he, Moses, showed no personal or selfish gain as he pled for the people.

God was pleased with his choice of the man Moses to lead His people. Moses was then told about the calf of gold.

17

Weeds and a Veil

Moses and Joshua started down the mountain and Joshua, military man that he was, claimed the camp had been attacked. "It's war!" he said, "There is a noise of war in the camp" (Exod. 32:17).

"No," Moses answered, "It's a revolt against God!"

True, this was not the sound of clashing swords or screams of dying and wounded men. There were yells, shouting, uncontrolled laughing, loud screams and wild, crashing noises. Thousands of voices filled the air with maddening, manmade thunder. This was idolatrous men and women gone mad.

Open rebellion was in full force and when the scene finally came within sight, even Moses was not prepared for what he saw. Here was a heathen spectacle of grotesque, distorted dancing, sexuality and indecency, excessive eating, gluttony and drinking with widespread drunkenness. Uncontrolled shouting, wild leaping in, around and through bonfires, lewd and other degrading acts spread throughout the entire camp. The roar was deafening. Its ear-shattering sounds could be heard for miles as it echoed against canyon walls and it centered around a calf made of gold. This was the height of pagan, uncivilized, degraded idolatry and it was all performed by the Israelite nation.

The rage of Moses burned hot within him. As he stood high above the scene, his face was red with fury. In his arms he clutched two tablets of God's law, written in stone by the finger of God Himself.

Everything stopped instantly when they saw him.

He was in a fit of rage. His eyes were like burning flames of fire as he roared at them. It was like thunder itself. Then, with his arms raised far above his head, and roaring with anger, he deliberately and violently hurled both tablets wildly over the heads of the idolaters smashing them to pieces at their feet. Both lay shattered in bits and pieces as some flew in all directions.

The stillness that followed was so thick it hurt. Faces just seconds before streaked with wild passion had suddenly gone chalk-white with fear.

Wailing broke the silence as people, thousands of them, threw themselves face down on the ground pounding it with clenched fists. Tears streamed down their faces, they raised their eyes and with screaming voices called to God for forgiveness.

They who promised obedience to the supreme God of the universe had openly broken their holy pledge. And now, because of their shameful, illicit acts they had broken His holy and solemn covenant. They had willingly broken all of God's laws. What were the results?

Moses pleaded forcefully with God to save their lives. With bitter tears he also begged God to spare the life of his brother. Remember God spared Cain's life who killed his brother Abel. Cain lived! Why did God do that? I believe God spared him to demonstrate to the world and the universe the result of rejecting God by wanting to do things their own way. Sin had risen its ugly head at Sinai through Satan. The hidden war started in heaven raged on.

Aaron's life was saved. He honestly repented with a complete and sincerely broken heart and God was willing to erase his sin through Christ. Following the destruction of the tablets and destroying the gold calf, Moses had the idol's metal remains ground into powder. Once this was done, he scattered the pulverized remains into the camp's drinking water. Then he ordered everyone to drink, thus putting an end to the rebellion and their so-called god.

What followed, however, was not a pretty sight. Ellen White describes the scene:

> Standing in the gate of the camp, Moses called to the people, "Who is on the Lord's side? let him come unto me." Those who had not joined in the apostasy were to take their position at the right of Moses; those who were guilty but repentant, at the left. The command was obeyed.
>
> It was found that the tribe of Levi had taken no part in the idolatrous worship. From among other tribes there were great numbers who, although they had sinned, now signified their repentance. But a large company, mostly of the mixed multitude that instigated the making of the calf, stubbornly persisted in their rebellion. In the name of "the Lord God of Israel," Moses now commanded those upon his right hand, who had kept themselves clear of idolatry, to gird on their swords and slay all who persisted in rebellion. "And there fell of the people that day about three thousand men." Without regard to position, kindred, or friendship, the ringleaders in wickedness were cut off; but all who repented and humbled themselves were spared. (Ibid., p. 324)

Many, with tears flowing down their faces, killed brothers, friends killed friends, fathers killed sons, and sons killed fathers. Not one guilty person was left alive. It was a horrible scene, but the idolatrous rebellion was stopped, and the mourning for the slain began. Families had been torn apart, loved ones were gone forever.

"Yet even here God's mercy was displayed. While He maintained His law, He granted freedom of choice and opportunity for repentance to all. Only those were cut off who persisted in rebellion" (Ibid., p. 325).

"Had these transgressors been spared, evils would have followed, greater than resulted from sparing the life of Cain. It was the mercy of God that thousands should suffer, to prevent the necessity of visiting judgments upon millions" (Ibid.).

If the Lord had withdrawn His protection entirely, the Israelite nation would have been weakened and God's name would have been laughed at and maybe even forgotten.

From all the stories Jesus told, there is one that Matthew, a disciple of Jesus, wrote. It is found in the thirteenth chapter of Matthew. This is what he recorded:

> The kingdom of heaven may be compared to a man who sowed [planted] good seed in his field; but while men were sleeping, his enemy came and sowed weeds among the wheat, and went away. So when the plants came up and bore [produced] grain, then the weeds appeared also. And the servants of the householder came and said to him, "Sir, did you not sow good seed in your field? How then has it weeds?" He said to them, "An enemy has done this." The servants said to him, "Then do you want us to go and gather them?" But he said, "No; lest in gathering the weeds you root up the wheat along with them. Let both grow together until the harvest; and at harvest time I will tell the reapers, Gather the weeds first and bind them in bundles to be burned, but gather the wheat into my barn." (Matt. 13:24–30, RSV)

Jesus was describing, this people, His church in the last days of earth's history. "Both classes are to be together in the church to the very end of time" (*The SDA Bible Commentary*, vol. 5, p. 408).

But what does this story have to do with what Moses just did? Thousands of people were put to death by his order. "The Redeemer does not want to lose one soul [person]; His experience with Judas is recorded to show His long patience with perverse human nature; and He bids us bear with it as He has borne. He has said that false brethren will be found in the church till the close of time" (*Christ's Object Lessons*, p. 73).

God and Moses waited patiently and long for the so-called "mixed multitude," the aliens and Egyptians that became members of the Israelite camp, to accept the true God. Most did not. Therefore, they were known as weeds among God's people. Fortunately, some were not weeds, but their numbers were small. This is why all were given a choice to stand with Moses. As a result of the weeds living among them, many Hebrews were contaminated to the extent that some accepted idolatry. This had to stop.

God's chosen people had to be pure to do His work. And being pure was not easy—then or now. A number of God's followers will always fail Him. But His true followers, although they may sin, choose to love and obey a God who also longs to forgive each and every one of them. No one can know the heart and mind of another human being. This is why weeds and wheat must grow together until the end of time—God's harvesting of the world.

Down through the centuries, and even today, many zealous professed Christians have thought it their duty to gather and burn, or otherwise persecute, those who they considered heretics. "But Christ has never committed such a task to His earthly representatives" (*The SDA Bible Commentary*, vol. 5, p. 408). Even with this statement we have an exception. "This is not to say that the church should take no action with regard to those whose lives or teachings already reveal the fruitage of evil" (Ibid.). Notice it said the church and not independent individuals. Carefully, with prayer, think that statement through.

When Moses came down from the mountain to the encampment after spending forty days with God, the people were awestruck by his appearance. This is one reason why they ran and hid. But why did they do this? It was because of what they saw on the face of Moses. The effect was blinding. It was almost like staring directly into the sun. No wonder people ran. The light streaming from his face was painful to look at. Their eyes hurt even from a quick glance (based on Exod. 34:29).

The strange part about this was that Moses himself didn't realize his face glowed like that. Finally, someone was brave enough to point at his face, then motion toward the sun. He got the message and found a covering to veil his face until the light eventually faded.

If someone were to look upon God's face they would not live. But, even though Moses talked with God in the cloud physically, he did not die. Exodus 33:20 reads "... there shall no man see me, and live." This statement is followed by verse 23 as it says, "... my face shall not be seen."

But what about Moses? He talked with God and lived. *Patriarchs and Prophets*, page 328, has this comment: "The unveiled glory of God, no man in this mortal state can look upon and live; but Moses was assured that he should behold as much of the divine glory as he could endure." Ellen White also says that it was because the life of Moses was in harmony with the will of his Maker that he stood in the presence of the Lord and was not afraid (Ibid., p. 329).

There must have been some kind of screening process to protect Moses from direct contact, otherwise he would not have survived. It is unbelievable to think of the enormous power that radiates from God's face alone. Moses didn't realize this, but the effects of his being that close with Him for all that time did have an effect. It was overpowering and the face of Moses had to be covered.

God truly is the Light of the world and throughout the universe as well.

18

Strange Fire

The wilderness tabernacle was portable and Moses was the key figure for its construction, working arrangement, and most important, its function. God personally directed him in the making of this hand-carried house of worship. He did it by giving Moses exact detailed information about its form and appearance. It had two compartments and all measurements had to be accurate to the smallest detail. Curtain hooks and sockets for holding posts upright were even discussed, and the meaning for its existence had to be clear. Nothing was left to chance (See Exod. 26 and 27).

A brief look at the finished product is important. One reason for its existence was to house the ark of the covenant. During its construction at Sinai these ex-slaves built the building from crafts learned in Egypt. Many were skilled artisans.

Besides it being easily transported, the building was magnificent. Its inner canvas sides became walls covered with pure gold. They glistened and shimmered with a soft glow. Curtains displayed splendid forms of angels in stimulating, vibrant colors of deep, rich shades. This was beautiful with a stunning rainbow effect. Flames leaped and flared from its exquisitely crafted altar and candelabras. As sacred fire filled the outer or first compartment with soft reflecting light, it flowed across gold lit walls, floors, dedicated furniture, and the ceiling itself.

In the second compartment, the Most Holy Place, rested the ark with its hovering, solid gold angels bowing above the brilliant glow of the mercy seat. Its beauty and glory can never be described. It is beyond imagination.

This and the fiery cloud suspended over the camp was God's home while among His people.

Aaron and two of his sons were officiating priests in this holy edifice. They were highly trained for their duties. Once inside the building, strict, orderly rules governed their every move. These men also must be pure, clean, with a complete attitude of reverence before entering.

But living unmolested on the Sinai plain made people content. Most liked it there. And a self-satisfied attitude crept in with the feeling of *why move?* This made them relaxed, content and sometimes careless or lazy. Thus, a feeling of pleasant satisfaction spread without the awareness of potential danger. They were settling down and forgetting their mission.

This attitude was also shared by Aaron's two sons, the ones who officiated in the tabernacle services. They became careless and self-assured of themselves and began drinking too much wine. One day, when they were completely drunk, it was their time to perform duties in the tabernacle's Holy Place.

Entering the building they became somewhat confused. And instead of using the holy fire that had been lit by God Himself for sacrificing, they used unsanctified or common fire. Instantly both men were ignited and died in flames.

Aaron had been watching their performance. And when this tragedy happened, he showed no emotion. He might have been screaming inside, but his face remained calm. He dared not show his feelings because he was standing on holy ground and Moses told him not to show grief lest the people should think that God was unjust.

Some of you who are reading this may not understand. In your mind you may be asking if God was just by His strictness. Eve thought the same thing when she was prevented from entering the garden, her home, after disobeying God. "Unfair," she complained to herself, "all I did was pick some fruit."

If God had overlooked the "strange fire" incident that Aaron's sons used, the sacredness of the tabernacle would have been weakened. It could have resulted in an attitude of *God will understand* or *what difference does it make, fire is fire?* This kind of thinking leads away from God's will. The attitude that God will understand and excuse their sin would take root and grow into rebellion.

Obeying God's rules and laws is no different today than when sacred duties were performed in the desert tabernacle. They need to be obeyed or nothing will work or survive. Yes, people make honest mistakes. All of us do. But one careless or intentional slip can be costly, as Aaron's sons found out.

Following the disaster of Aaron's sons, the cloud was seen moving away from Sinai and Moses gave orders to follow. There was a grumbling, resistance, and questions but they packed up anyway and began moving out.

If one were to close his or her eyes and picture that entire nation of Israelites on the move, what would it look like? Some travelers would be mournful, not because of the physical move or the journey ahead. No, they were leaving loved ones behind in the arms of death. Some may have been anxious for what problems lay ahead or just maybe tired of wandering not knowing where they were going. Others would grumble, thinking and asking where and when this would all end. Whatever the reasons, joyful or sad, they followed orders, all of them, and moved on.

It was like a river ever moving, except they were not a river of water, instead it was a flow of people flooding across the countryside. Babies in arms, old people riding in carts pulled by strong young men or maybe animals, and there were sheep, goats, cattle all raising voices and dust against prodding herdsmen. They too didn't know what the next stop would be. It was not quiet, especially with children laughing, crying, chasing one another, or playing games among the sounds of cattle.

And in the center of that moving river of humanity were priests dressed in long flowing robes of white. They were the ones who carried the holy ark of the covenant.

And ahead the cloud led the way. If the weather was hot, the cloud spread shade. At night it was light and heat. Whatever the need, it was filled because God traveled with them.

Others also, spies from enemy nations, were close or among them, sent to watch their every move. So it went as enemies lurked behind rocks or stood on cliffs reporting to nearby fearful cities. They knew what the Hebrew God had done and they trembled wondering if they too would feel His might. And so went the road leading away from Sinai.

As they advanced, the way became more difficult. Their route lay through stony ravines and barren waste. All around them was the great wilderness. There were those, as always, who questioned why travel "… a land of drought and of the shadow of death, through a land that no man passed through and where no man lived?" (Jer. 2:6, MEV).

"Their progress was necessarily slow and toilsome; and the multitudes, after their long encampment, were not prepared to endure the perils and discomforts of the way" (Ibid., p. 377). Complaining began after three days of this kind of travel. Trouble was brewing.

Yet, in spite of this, manna continued to fall every morning and the protecting cloud never went away. They murmured anyway. But they would have complained even louder if they knew what lay ahead.

19

Meat

They had plenty to eat, but manna was not what they wanted. "*Meat!* We want meat!" was the cry. And, as usual, the demands started from followers and hangers-on in the camp, the Egyptians and mixed multitude (Num. 11:4; *Patriarchs and Prophets*, pp. 377, 379).

Actually, they were not blaming Moses for not supplying meat to eat, they were accusing God instead. They insisted they should have meat. In reality, they were telling God they knew better about what food was right and best for their health and wellbeing. God had abundantly and lovingly supplied manna every morning. In supplying this kind of food, He was providing the right nutrition they vitally needed. As a result, there was not a sick, weak, or ailing person among that large body of people (Deut. 7:15).

Demands for meat grew stronger. Sharp complaints and murmuring about painful traveling conditions with only manna to eat erupted among all the tribes. Thoughts of *Will this nightmare ever end?* became stronger with each agonizing step they took.

All had agreed to obey God's authority, but now with the mixed multitude agitating everyone, a full-fledged rebellion was in the making. As the unrest spread, Moses became agitated. What could he do?

As always, Moses appealed to God and God gave them meat. He announced to Moses that He would send meat until they were sick of it.

And it would not be just for a day, a week or for several weeks; they would have enough for a full month's supply. "Their murmuring was now rebellion, and as such it [they] must receive prompt and signal punishment, if Israel was to be preserved from anarchy [having no government or law] and ruin" (*Patriarchs and Prophets*, p. 379).

Quail, by the thousands, flew into their nets. But what followed is one of God's strange acts. Before that took place, however, let's consider this. "Had they been willing to deny appetite, in obedience to His wise restrictions, feebleness and disease would have been unknown …. They would have had clear perceptions of truth and duty, keen discrimination, and sound judgment" (Ibid., p. 378).

But they wanted their way and they got it. Thus, "… their unwillingness to submit to the restrictions and requirements of God, prevented them, to a great extent, from reaching the high standard which He desired them to attain …" (Ibid.).

So what did God do?

Along with abundant meat came fire. He flashed lightning bolts from the cloud causing flames as rain to fall on the camp and run along the ground. Many died, especially the ringleaders with their rebellious demands. The fire stopped only when Moses pleaded with God to end His disastrous action. Once again, the love of Moses for the chosen people of God was felt by God Himself, and He took the fire away, but sickness remained behind which had been unknown before. It spread quickly among the tribes (*Patriarchs and Prophets*, p. 379).

Although these people were God's representatives to a fallen world, they had listened to Satan's lies as did Eve centuries before. This had to stop. Thus, God stepped in and performed another of His strange acts.

History reveals those strange acts. They have been seen in such events as Noah's flood, Lot's wife turning to a pillar of salt, the sufferings of Job and Samson losing his strength. Yet every action by God, great or small, is real. And they are recorded for our benefit.

Why, yes why, one may ask, does He do this? It is because the earth and its people are still in an ongoing war. It is that civil war which erupted in heaven. The fighting is still going on. The battlefield is not in heaven any longer because the action is now centered, transferred to the confines of each and every beat of the human heart.

The rebellion that faced Moses over the meat issue was not all, no, there was more to come. After leaving Taberah, where the cry for meat took place, their next stop was Hazeroth. It was here that Aaron and Miriam made a grab for power. As if Moses didn't have enough on his hands, now his own family was questioning his authority to lead the Israelite nation (See Num. 11).

Miriam did not like the wife of Moses, Zipporah. She was jealous, calling her an outsider and not an Israelite. But that was far from the truth. Zipporah was a descendent of Abraham, as was Miriam, and both worshiped the same God. Miriam also accused her of being from a different race because of her dark skin. Worst of all, Miriam and Aaron both contested that they should have as much or even more power than Moses because God had talked with each one of them as He did with their brother (Num. 12:1; *Patriarchs and Prophets*, p. 383).

This kind of thinking reeked of rebellion and if it did not stop, the entire camp would be forced to choose sides. This was Satan's plan to separate, divide and destroy God's chosen people. God stepped in and called all three—Moses, Aaron, and Miriam—to come to the tent of meetings, the portable tabernacle.

Once there, hidden in the cloud, He told them strongly that Moses, not either of the two of them, was His appointed leader. "This manifestation of the Lord's displeasure was designed to be a warning to all Israel, to check the growing spirit of discontent and insubordination" (Ibid., p. 385).

An important statement follows this last quote and its application is for everyone in every age and time of this world's history. Here is what it says. "Envy is one of the most satanic traits that can exist in the human heart, and it is one of the most baleful [deadly] in its effects" (Ibid.). "For where envying and strife is, there is confusion and every evil work" (James 3:16).

What was the reaction of Moses to these accusations by his brother and sister? He was silent and uncomplaining. This was a patient, humble,

God-loving man. His attitude, or quality of character, had been developed slowly by long years, forty of them in all, while living in a lonely wilderness herding sheep and goats. This condition that was perfected by God had not come easy for him or developed overnight.

The action on the part of Miriam and Aaron had to be dealt with. All the nation was watching for the outcome. If unchecked or ignored their action would open a door for more of the same. "God had chosen Moses, and had put His spirit upon him; and Miriam and Aaron, by their murmurings, were guilty of disloyalty, not only to their appointed leader, but to God Himself" (*Patriarchs and Prophets*, pp. 384, 385).

Since Miriam was the main one who led this rebellion, she was the one to suffer most. Instantly she was covered with the deadly disease called leprosy. She screamed in pain. The Bible says she was as white as snow (Num. 12:10). Aaron was not punished. His penalty was to see his sister in that dreadful condition. He with bitter, humble tears confessed their sin. He pleaded for God to cure his sister. Moses also prayed deeply and passionately for his sister to be restored.

God did hear their prayers. Miriam sincerely repented with agonizing tears and God removed the disease. But she had been banished from the camp for seven days before that happened. God even withdrew His presence from the tabernacle.

What a blessing and relief it was for both God and Moses when Miriam and Aaron honestly confessed their evil deeds and fully, completely repented.

We have seen many unusual things in this story, but one thing stands out. It is very clear God was not finished with them with His strong acts of punishments for strong acts of rebellion. Not just yet. There were more to come as we shall see, and I might add, even in our day.

20

Kadesh

The cloud began to move again and the nation of nomads followed. As they approached the Kadesh border, tension grew. This was not the tension of rebellion. No, they were feelings of excitement and anxiety and there was good reason for this. The Promised Land was almost within sight. As the saying goes, they could almost taste and smell the end of their nightmarish travels.

> *As they approached the Kadesh border, tension grew. This was not the tension of rebellion. No, they were feelings of excitement and anxiety and there was good reason for this. The Promised Land was almost within sight.*

Talk was loud as people gathered in groups. There was much arm-raising and handclapping. These worn out, weary wanderers electrified themselves as they talked loudly together. They were almost home.

Questions circulated wildly such as, "What does the place look like? Is the land good? Will it grow food? What about the people who live there, are they few or many, strong or weak?" Moses was almost mobbed. Thousands were talking to him all at once. They wanted answers.

He withdrew to talk with God, then his advisors. Eventually a decision emerged to secretly send men as spies to look the land over and report back what they saw. Twelve were chosen, one from each tribe. Cautioned to use extreme care they were instructed to bring proof that the land was everything they hoped for. This was a bold plan involving danger, yet all twelve were willing and eager to risk the hazards. They left in high spirits.

The camp was unusually quiet while the men were gone. No one complained. Day after day the twelve men with their secret mission were all they could think or talk about. Routine chores were done, meals prepared, washing taken care of and children were more obedient than usual. Prayers were offered for the safety of the twelve. Yet, all the while, they kept wondering what kind of a report the spies would bring back.

One week went by, then two. The third brought anxiety. Where were they? What took them so long? Deep concern followed on the fourth week. But as day forty arrived a shout went up from the hills. There they were! All twelve of them! They were safe, and they were back!

People acting as children went running. They shoved, pushed and a few strong words filled the air as each crowded close around Moses and the twelve spies. They strained to hear every word of the report. After all, this was to be their future and they wanted to hear about it.

And what a glowing report it was. The twelve had explored the entire area, almost every inch of it, even inspecting its produce. As proof, they brought back a huge cluster of grapes. It was so heavy it took two men to carry it on a pole between them. Truly this was a land flowing with milk and honey. Eagerly, they hung on to every word. They were breathless and overtaken with emotion.

But then came the bad news. The people living on the land were powerful. Their strength and cities were secure behind well-fortified walls so strong that it would be impossible to conquer them. And there were huge giants, armed and ready to defend themselves.

Of the twelve men only two, Joshua and Caleb, said, and it was Caleb who said it, "Let us go up at once and possess it [the land], for we are well able to overcome" (Num. 13:30).

The other ten shouted, "NO, WE CAN'T!" The people listened to and believed the ten. Instantly, everyone turned from jubilation to deep anguish and disappointment. They moaned.

Murmuring erupted again as shouting and wailing followed. Cries were heard such as, "Why did we leave Egypt for this?" and "What is God doing to us now?" They accused Moses and God both of leading them into the desert for nothing.

Moses and Aaron knew that these people were not ready for possessing the Promised Land. "Revolt and open mutiny quickly followed; for Satan had full sway, and the people seemed bereft [lacking] of reason. They cursed Moses and Aaron, forgetting that God hearkened [listened] to their wicked speeches, and that, enshrouded [hidden] in the cloudy pillar, the Angel of His presence was witnessing their terrible outburst of wrath" (*Patriarchs and Prophets*, p. 389).

Yes, God was watching and listening.

Moses and Aaron went face down on the ground in prayer as Caleb and Joshua desperately pled with the people to believe them and change their minds, to stop their unbelief and trust God. People were ready to stone Moses and his brother. Suddenly and without warning, the presence of the Lord appeared at the tabernacle. Moses stopped praying immediately and entered the sacred tent.

Here again we learn what kind of man Moses was. His true identity revealed itself. As he and God talked inside that holy place of worship, the Lord showed His displeasure. He was about to destroy the entire nation by producing another race of people through Moses and start over again.

Moses pleaded "No! These are Your people!"

He begged God not to go through with what He had just said. He reminded Him who didn't need reminding that these were His people, and to please forgive them once more.

Moses went on to add that if He did this, the Egyptians and other nations would say He was not able to do as He said He would by giving freedom and the land of their enemies to a nation of slaves.

Moses loved God's chosen people, the Israelites, and he offered himself and his future if only God would spare them. He was not thinking of himself, he was thinking of others, those rebellious people camping outside the tabernacle. There was not one selfish attitude in this man. He was continually thinking of others.

As a response, the Lord did forgive the Israelites, but—and that one word had a sting in it—there would be a set of rules, terms, and final conditions. Because of their unbelief and cowardice, He would not show His power to dislodge their enemies and give them the land He promised. Instead, they would only be safe if *they turned back to the Red Sea.*

This group of people, the Israelites, were special. And that word special does not accurately describe who they really were. We can only say they were the only large number of men, women, young people, and children who knew just who the real God of heaven and earth was. That made them different, special from all others in the human family. God always had His so-called special people from the moment time began. But now He took these people, under the leadership of Moses, and began preparing them for a vital mission, to tell and show the world who He, God, was. And as always, Satan was right there to try and stop it.

So, here we go again, a setback in the training of God's people and it would not be the last time either. The seeds of discontent were still embedded in them. They were smoldering, ready to erupt. God and Moses both knew it. There would be more defiant actions by His chosen people in the future, and it was not far off.

But God's punishment for their rebellious attitude to the spies' report was not over. He continued, and Joshua and Caleb were excluded from what He was about to say. There were others also, such as the Levite tribe, that had been loyal and thus were also exempt.

God announced that because of their unbelief, all the men over the age of twenty would die in the wilderness. And there would be a forty-year period of wandering in the desert ahead of them all. The forty-year number corresponded with the forty days the spies had been away to survey the Promised Land.

Reaction to this was instant. There was sincere repentance by the masses of Israelites. Yet even then, not all were of that decision because there were those who refused to accept God's announcement. They took matters into their own hands. They decided to fight and take the Promised Land by force, either with or without God and Moses. They tried, failed, and of course were slaughtered.

This action caused problems for the Hebrews in the future because of the victory by the nations occupying the land of promise. The victors became arrogant and smug. So instead of fearing the Israelite nation and its God, as they once had, they now felt themselves invincible and superior. The Israelites that survived the battle of the rebels still did not like what they heard from God, and some were determined to do something about it.

It is amazing that after all they had seen, heard and been through, even being defeated by fierce fighting, they could still think such things. They should have realized also that God was close by, within reach so to speak, watching over every move they made.

Fortunately, not everyone went along with the negative frame of mind found in others. "In commanding them to retire from the land of their enemies, God tested their apparent submission and proved that it was not real" (*Patriarchs and Prophets*, p. 391).

Licking the wounds of their recent defeat, those rebellious Israelites nurtured a deep-rooted resentment. A plan to revolt was brewing. They felt they would yet find a way to overthrow the authority of their leaders, especially Moses—who they also knew was appointed by God—and take his power of leadership away from him. This was a plan formed by Satan.

There was trouble ahead.

21

Korah

Korah was highly respected, an important man from the tribe of Levi. He was a cousin of Moses. He was responsible for duties directly connected with the tabernacle.

Besides Korah, there were two other men, Dathan and Abiram who claimed to be direct descendants of Jacob's first-born son, Reuben. This they felt gave them the right to be eligible and part of the official, civil leadership of the Hebrew nation.

These men, along with Korah, began a strong movement to remove Moses from his position. Another man named On was also involved, but he apparently withdrew from the plot when he saw its true nature and motives. Korah was jealous of Moses and longed for his position. He felt himself better qualified to lead the Israelites than was Moses. He reasoned he could take the nation safely and in triumph into the Promised Land by subduing it. Korah was not only jealous, but greed for power possessed his every thought. His was an evil plan to create unrest and dissatisfaction by opposing God's two appointed leaders, Moses and Aaron. He was gaining followers rapidly.

Rebellion raised its ugly head again. The deceptive lessons of jealousy and power-grabbing had not been learned by the events with Miriam. This movement was far worse, however, than was that of Miriam. This time it involved the very top leaders of the Hebrew people. It spoke of rebellion against the authority of God. It was an "I have my rights" campaign. It echoed of the sin and evil mind of Lucifer's demands in heaven.

The official leaders from each tribe had the title of prince. The total count was 250 and Korah's scheming mind, a prince with appealing ways, won hundreds of followers. "Why are we not in the Promised Land?" many asked. "God promised He would give it to us. Now it's back to the desert for forty years. *NEVER!* This is Moses' doing, and his alone!"

Mutiny and defiant revolt sounded loud and clear. It was digging deep into the minds of thousands. Korah, the traitor led by Satan, was winning. Yet as before, not all were convinced. Thousands still knew and trusted Moses. He had been a kind leader, patient, fair, self-sacrificing, and above all a true man of God. God was first in his life, even before his own wants. He loved these people and they said so to those in rebellion. But the rebels claimed the only purpose of Moses for leading them out of Egypt was to rob them of their possessions and leave them destitute or dead in the wilderness.

And where was Moses all this time? What was he doing? He was, as always, doing the work God asked him to do. He led, judged, kept records, and performed duties at the tabernacle whenever his counsel and presence were asked for or needed.

Meanwhile, Korah, assuming the people were with him, fearlessly "… and publicly accused Moses and Aaron of usurping authority which Korah and his associates were equally entitled to share" (*Patriarchs and Prophets*, p. 398). He also "… charged, further, that the people had been deprived of their liberty and independence. 'Ye take [grab] too much [power] upon you …'" (Ibid.). Then adding muscle to his statements, he boldly added "… seeing all the congregation are holy, every one of them, and the Lord is among them: wherefore [why] then lift ye up yourselves above the congregation of the Lord?" (Ibid.).

What was the reaction of Moses? "Moses had not suspected this deep-laid plot, and when its terrible significance burst upon him, he fell upon his face [prostrated himself] in silent appeal to God" (Ibid.).

Did God hear him? "He [Moses] arose sorrowful indeed, but calm and strong. Divine guidance had been granted him. 'Even tomorrow,' he said, 'the Lord will show who are His, and who is holy; and will cause him to come near unto Him: even him whom He hath chosen will He cause to come near unto Him'" (Ibid.).

This statement is of vital significance. God and the reaction of Moses were one in the same. A major rebellion, actually treason, not only exploded against Moses, but also against God Himself. They were accusing both, especially God, of being unfair. God could have destroyed them right then and there for this, but no, He gave them space, a day of time to reflect upon what they were doing. And if they repented of their accusations, He was willing to work with them and forgive their actions. Moses agreed to settle the rebellion the next day, not only because he was told to do so by God, but because it was his way of life to obey and not act in haste or from temper.

Moses was also quick to observe that Dathan and Abiram were not as bold or defiant as was Korah. But there was no hesitation on the part of Korah, their leader. His actions were fearless and belligerent as he continued to accuse Moses of wrongdoing.

Moses sent word that he wished to talk with both Dathan and Abiram. His thinking was that maybe, just maybe, they could quietly discuss things together. He wanted to make a try and reason with them about their wrong. It was crystal clear that God had appointed Moses as their leader and from all the evidence these two men had seen in the past, there should have been no doubt or question as to who God chose to represent Him.

Dathan and Abiram refused to talk with Moses.

God and Moses had offered time for these men to reconsider their actions. Instead, they took this opportunity to discredit Moses by saying he was nothing more than an evil tyrant. And within hearing of the people, both blamed Moses for not living in the Promised Land now, and it was his plan to return them to forty years of wandering in the desert.

Satan was showing his power. It was both clever and deceitful to misrepresent that Moses was following his own selfish interests and not being lead by God in order induce the Israelites to join the rebellion. The rebel leaders were jealously focused on serving their own self interests (does that sound familiar?) and Satan was determined to give them what they wanted to fill his purpose no matter what.

Sadly, the majority of the Israelites accepted this radical opinion. Satan knew these people were tired and worn out from what they had gone through and he was using this fact to his advantage. In the meantime, tomorrow, the day of grace, was looming closer.

Moses asked the princes, all 250 of them to bring their censers to the tabernacle the next day. This was of vital importance.

A censer is a cup-like container for burning incense. It is usually covered with small holes on the lid and carried by hand on long, thin chains. During religious ceremonies, the censer is swung by the chains and waved back and forth to spread the smoking odor of incense. Burning coals were taken from the top of the altar outside the tabernacle, placed in these censers and used in the services.

Smoke from these censers represented the prayers of God's followers, His loyal and faithful people, a symbol of devotion and loyalty ascending continually to heaven. This was physical evidence asking for guidance, forgiveness, instruction, and a show of gratitude. This was to affirm their deep devotion and love for His care and goodness.

On the following day, the princes were to bring their censers for the precise purpose of learning just who God had chosen to lead His people. This was to be done in faith. But that night—the night of their probation—the accusers were not spending time in prayer, asking for pardon, forgiveness, and guidance. Instead, the hours were spent in feelings of resentment against God's chosen leaders and their authority and they silently formed plans to kill both Moses and Aaron.

Thus, the following morning, Korah encouraged the entire congregation of Israel to gather near the tabernacle to watch for the announcement from God as to who His appointed leaders were.

Moses called for the censers to be lit, all 250 of them. A procession of high-ranking men of intelligence, power and leadership stepped forward. One by one they took coals from the altar in the courtyard and lit their censers (Num. 16:17, 19).

In answer to their prayers that ascended up to heaven with their incense, the glory of God was displayed. He asked Moses and Aaron to step aside from Korah and the others. He was about to destroy them all. The two men did not step aside. Instead they lay prostrate and with tears rolling down his face, Moses pled with God not to do His strange act. He and Aaron continued pleading with every fiber of strength in their bodies. "No, God, please don't destroy everyone because of these men" (Num. 16:19–21).

God spoke directly to Moses. Upon hearing His words and decision, Moses arose and with the seventy loyal elders that were with him, went forward to pronounce the divine judgment.

Korah had walked over to stand with Dathan and Abiram. Moses spoke to all three from a distance, asking them to recant. He pled with them. They refused.

Following God's own direction and instruction, Moses then told everyone to step back and away from the rebellious leaders. They were to touch nothing these people owned, for if they did, they would suffer the same fate as them for the sins these men committed. They did so in haste and terror. Yet the ringleaders of the movement, with their families, stood as defiant as ever.

Following this, Moses made an announcement. It was loud and clear.

> Hereby ye shall know that the Lord hath sent me to do all these works; for I have not done them of mine own mind. If these men die the common death [a natural death] of all men, or if they be visited after the visitation [punishment] of all men, then the Lord hath not sent me. But if the Lord make a new thing [do something unusual], and the earth open her mouth, and swallow them up, with all that appertain unto them [everything that belongs to them], and they go down quick into the pit [grave], then ye shall understand that these men have provoked the Lord. (*Patriarchs and Prophets*, p. 400)

As Moses finished speaking there was a rumbling sound. Screaming and shouting erupted from thousands of throats. Fear marked every face.

Panic followed. A wild, uncontrolled human stampede pushed, shoved, and knocked each other down. People fainted. And regardless of who and what age they were, others trampled on one another in their desperate attempt to escape. There was widespread fear among young and old alike.

Great clouds of dust arose in the air as people in vast numbers ran for their lives. The ground had split. It ripped wide open right beneath Korah, Dathan, Abiram, and all their families. Their unearthly screaming along with everything they owned completely disappeared from sight. It was a horrible hour of indescribable terror. Then suddenly, and as quickly as it had snapped open, the ground slammed shut on those once healthy men, women, and children.* They were lost forever beneath the ground. All of them died.

Flaming tongues of fire suddenly shot out of the cloud and consumed all 250 princes. They had not died with Korah and the leaders of the rebellion. These men were saved to witness the consequences of rebellion against God. By saving them from Korah's fate, God was offering another chance to repent, but they did not. Still sympathizing with the rebels, they shared their fate by instant death.

(Note: The censers of the princes were made of silver. They had held sacred fire from the altar and burned incense. These were gathered up, melted, and formed into a covering for the altar in the outer courtyard of the tabernacle).

But there were yet others who were in sympathy with the rebels. These were still given a chance to recant. "But while they fled from the judgments, through fear of destruction, their rebellion was not cured. They returned to their tents that night terrified, but not repentant" (Ibid., p. 401).

They had been convinced that Moses had wronged them. And if they now stated that Moses was right and led by God, they would have to accept the fact that most of them would die in the wilderness during the next forty years. They convinced themselves that Korah and his people had been right, and they also concluded that Moses, somehow, had caused their deaths.

The rebellion was not over yet.

Once again, God, by giving them a night to think things through was allowing time, a trial period, to repent. But instead of taking those precious hours to examine carefully and accept the words of God by Moses, they made plans to kill him. Numbers 16:41 tells what happened the following morning: "But on the morrow all the congregation of the children of Israel murmured against Moses and against Aaron, saying, 'Ye have killed the people of the LORD.'"

Following the utterance of these words, the cloud was seen again over the tent of the tabernacle. And from deep within it came a death sentence for Israel. Moses fell flat on the ground praying and knowing this death sentence was then and now racing among the people. He shouted to Aaron, "RUN! Run among the people. Run, Aaron! Take a censer and *GO!* RUN as fast as you can!"

Taking a censer, Aaron ran swinging his smoking censer and plunged into the midst of that great mass of people. In the meantime, Moses was still in deep prayer pleading for God's people. And God answered him by stopping the race of death among the people. And there stood Aaron in their midst, still swinging the burning censer between the dead on one side and the living on the other (Num. 16:46, 47).

All told, the death count of the rebellion of Korah numbered more than 15,000 people. "For if we sin deliberately after receiving the knowledge of the truth, there no longer remains a sacrifice for sins" (Heb. 10:26, RSV). And God sadly says, "[L]et him [them] alone" (Hosea 4:17, RSV).

There was more convincing and concluding evidence to come. God had indeed chosen Moses and Aaron as His leaders. A rod was called for from each of the twelve tribes with their name written on each one, respectively. Moses wrote Aaron's name on the Levi rod for the tribe of Levi. This was because there was no prince to represent that tribe. These rods were then placed in the tabernacle, "before the testimony" (Num. 17:4). The rod that blossomed on the following day was God's announcement that it was His choice for the tribe who would become His priesthood.

The next morning the rod that blossomed was the one from the tribe of Levi with Aaron's name on it. It not only blossomed, it had buds and flower blossoms with ripe almonds. This rod was set aside and stored in the tabernacle as evidence. It settled forever the question of the priesthood.

It was a quiet and subdued nation that looked across the desert. This was to be their home for the next forty years as a whole generation would die off. And they did not look forward to it. Tents came down and were packed away. Household belongings were loaded onto carts. Cattle, sheep, and goats were herded for travel as thousands of downhearted nomads left the scene of terrible devastation behind.

As they moved away, clouds of dust rose high in the air behind them. It was hot as the heat from sand-scorched miles began to trail behind them. They were headed in the direction of the Red Sea. And no one wanted to go there.

What about Moses, what was he thinking now?

He and God had been through so much together. There had been tears for both of them, many tears. Proof for that is clear. God gave His lost loved ones, even Korah, so many chances to come back to Him. And however hard it was for Him, God would respect their choices, their wishes, and decisions as He did with Lucifer. The results of His strange acts were never easy on Him. Yet they had to be done. But there still remained others loyal to Him to protect and guide. This battle with Satan had been sadly won, and both God and Moses knew there would be more.

So now what of Moses? What would he do? There is no question about his future actions. He would continue to do what he had always done. He would obey and follow whatever his Friend God asked him to do. Hand in hand they would lead as before, right on into the heart of those forty years in that burning wilderness waste of endless desert.

> *The next morning the rod that blossomed was the one from the tribe of Levi with Aaron's name on it. It not only blossomed, it had buds and flower blossoms with ripe almonds. This rod was set aside and stored in the tabernacle as evidence. It settled forever the question of the priesthood.*

*A special note.

Questions have been raised from time to time as to why God destroyed small children in such cases as that of Korah. In my research I ran across an interesting passage concerning that very question in *The SDA Bible Commentary*, vol. 1, page 877. It reads as follows,

"The root word translated 'little children' [as mentioned in connection with Korah in Numbers 16:27] means 'to take quick steps,' 'to trip along,' and refers to children who are old enough to walk about safely on their own. The same word is used in 2 Chronicles. 20:12; 31:18. God did not impose this death penalty upon small children. But, as often happens, innocent children suffered for the obstinacy of their elders, who refuse to repent or even to heed the warning to flee. Some at least of Korah's children survived (Num. 26:11; Exod. 6:24)."

Numbers 26:11 reads, "Notwithstanding the children of Korah died not." And *The SDA Bible Commentary*, vol. 1, page 918 has this note for that verse: "The children of Korah. They continued to have a good name even in David's time, and did not perish as did the descendants of Dathan and Abiram. The Korathites, a subdivision of the Levites, constituted one of the temple choirs."

Exodus 6:24 reads, "And the sons of Korah; Assir, and Elkanah, and Abiasaph: these are the families of the Korhites." And the commentary on this verse reads, "Not all of the sons of Korah were destroyed with their father in the uprising in the desert .... The three sons mentioned here became heads of 'families of the Korhites' whose descendants were famous as temple singers in David's time" (Ibid., p. 526).

22

Ten Times Four-XL

[T]hou in thy great mercies didst not forsake them in the wilderness; the pillar of cloud which led them in the way did not depart from them by day, nor the pillar of fire by night which lighted for them the way by which they should go. Thou gavest thy good Spirit to instruct them, and didst not withhold thy manna from their mouth, and gavest them water for their thirst. Forty years didst thou sustain them in the wilderness, and they lacked nothing; their clothes did not wear out and their feet did not swell. (Neh. 9:19–21, RSV)

This forty-year period is to some degree lost to us. The Bible record is sparse. We can make educated guesses as to what they did and how they lived. We do know, however, they traveled extensively, but to where and when is still somewhat of a mystery. Many thought because of the revolt of Korah God had abandoned them. That is not true. The presence of the cloud told them God had not gone away. The fact of a continual supply of manna and water told them He was supplying their daily needs. And Moses was still leading them. These people were not constantly being attacked by enemies. God cared. He always did, and in time they would realize He always would.

Here again, God was training a people for what lay ahead. Simply, He was sifting the wheat from the tares (noxious weeds), the true believers from those who were not, such as the tag-along crowds. And it was taking a very long, long time to do so.

During that time the younger generation was growing to adulthood. The older were dying off as predicted. But even then the seeds of rebellion had not been completely destroyed. They simply lay dormant. Satan knew this and was simply biding his time creating plans for the right opportunity to show itself for spreading his evil. He too was playing the waiting game.

There is evidence for this. We know of two instances when things flared up. One time a man deliberately worked on Sabbath. He went out during the sacred hours to hunt for and collect firewood, then he lit a fire. This was directly against God's express command. Moses was consulted. He immediately took the case before the Lord. The sentence was death by stoning outside the camp area.

Another offense was when a man of Egyptian descent moved his tent into an Israelite camp. This was forbidden. He claimed to have a perfect right to do so because his mother was an Israelite even though his father was Egyptian. When he and an Israelite man got into a fight, the man exploded in a rage of temper and cursed God. He was taken to Moses. Moses didn't know what to do with him. Thus, he was held until God was consulted. The sentence, by divine command, was death. He had committed blasphemy when he cursed God and he was stoned to death outside the camp.

Such things as these, along with other problems usually came from what is termed the mixed multitude. These were non-Israelites who joined the Hebrew nation. They claimed to have accepted Israel's God, but their years of idolatry, in most cases, had never completely left them or their way of thinking.

Water in desert wastelands is almost an unknown. It was no different when the Israelites wandered in those barren places. The need was great and it took a tremendous amount of water to satisfy the daily needs of thousands. Besides that, we can't forget the animal herds and flocks as well. So, where did all of it come from? In Nehemiah 9:20 we learn it was God who supplied that vital element.

Let's skip over now to the ending of the forty-year period of wandering. As mentioned, God had produced an unending amount of running water for their every need. It flowed beside their encampment. But now, almost within sight of the Canaan hills, that flow dried up and stopped.

The long years of wandering had almost come to an end. It had not been easy. Many loved ones had been left behind. Fathers, mothers, brothers, sisters, friends all lay beneath the sands of the desert. But now with the Promised Land within reach, their spirits sprang to a high level of happiness. They were almost home.

> *The long years of wandering had almost come to an end. It had not been easy. Many loved ones had been left behind. Fathers, mothers, brothers, sisters, friends all lay beneath the sands of the desert. But now with the Promised Land within reach, their spirits sprang to a high level of happiness. They were almost home.*

But as the water supply dried up and there was nothing to drink, a crisis arose. They always had water. It was taken for granted that God would supply it no matter how dry a place might be.

Now, at Kadesh where they camped, there was no water. They complained to Moses. "We need water," they told him, "and we need it now!" Moses explained that since they were near the land of Edom, where Esau's descendants lived, there would be water, plenty of it. The land was well saturated with more water than they could ever want and there was an abundant supply of food also. They could buy both and then continue traveling through Esau's land to Canaan. This was God's plan (Num. 20; *Patriarchs and Prophets*, p. 413).

Moses also reminded them of God's promise to protect them as they traveled. He then added that the Edomites were actually afraid of them and they would not be molested for any reason. But their reaction to all this was unbelief plus a total lack of faith. They didn't look back to the miracles God had done for them in the past. Instead, in this a first of many tests to come, they failed completely. Bitter complaining followed. They brought up long-forgotten grudges by saying they wished they had died in the rebellion of Korah. "Now!" they shouted at Moses, "you brought us here to die!" The seeds of rebellion, dormant for so long, had sprouted. Satan was dancing for joy. It was the chance he was waiting for.

Leaders of this movement rushed to the tabernacle and prostrated themselves (stretched flat on the ground, with faces down on the soil) pleading with God for water. As a result, God spoke to Moses saying, "Take the rod [his staff], and gather thou the assembly together, thou, and Aaron thy brother, and speak ye unto the rock before their eyes; and it shall give forth his water, and thou shalt bring forth to them water out of the rock: so thou shalt give the congregation and their beasts drink" (Num. 20:8).

The instructions were clear and simple enough. God was about to grant their wish. But something had gone drastically wrong. Oh yes, the water gushed out all right as promised, lots of it. But that was not the situation. It was Moses who was the problem this time. He did not do as God asked him to do. He knew what God asked him to do. But when hordes of people rushed on him with violence demanding water .... Yes, he was their leader. So, they automatically turned to him for answers and help with all their problems.

They had chosen him to be their leader at the time God's voice spoke directly to them and now they accused him for the lack of water. What was he going to do about it? Something snapped inside Moses.

Taking Aaron with him they rushed to the specified rock. In a fit of anger he did not speak to it. Instead he raised his staff of authority and violently pounded the stone. He did it twice shouting, "Hear now, ye rebels [meaning the startled thousands watching him]; must we fetch you water out of this rock?" (Num. 20:10). As a result of his temper, water did burst from the rock and all were satisfied. It was a powerful flow.

The word "WE" and striking the rock twice was the sin of Moses. By saying "we," he was indicating that he and his brother preformed the miracle, not God. True, most all of those people were rebels and tried his patience to the breaking point. God told Moses to only speak to the rock, but Moses hit it twice. After all those years he had fallen apart. This points out that he was human with passions and impatience instead of righteous indignation. God's chosen leader had claimed credit for the water. God had been left out. To those watching, it indicated that God could not perform the miracle and that Moses did. This was wrong and he knew it the instant he said "we."

Leadership is hard on anyone, even Moses. Now what? His rashness may have been just the thing some people and Satan were looking for, a flaw in his leadership. Now they could say he was not fit to lead the Israelites into the Promised Land.

Moses was an old man by now and time was taking its toll. He was worn out, yet strong and powerful as ever. God saw to that. But for this act there was no excuse. By this act, he proved that the human family is a fallen race capable, without exception, of sinning. Moses instantly knew what he had done. Full of agonizing pain, with tears flowing down his face he, with Aaron, rushed to the tabernacle falling prostrate pleading for forgiveness.

Thousands were watching. What would God do?

God spoke. He told both that He would not now let them lead His people into the Promised Land. This almost destroyed Moses. After all they had been through together. God was his closest and dearest Friend. Now this! The land of promise was almost within sight. Now Moses and Aaron were destined to not enter, but the people would cross into it. This may appear as cruel and harsh treatment. But both accepted the penalty without complaint. "But in the light of Bible history it is evident that God's goodness and His love engage [causes] Him to deal with sin as an evil fatal to the peace and happiness of the universe" (*Patriarchs and Prophets*, p. 420).

It was a small thing that Moses did. "Moses was not guilty of a great crime, as men would view the matter; his sin was one of common occurrence .... To human judgment this may seem a light thing; but if God dealt so severely with this sin in His most faithful and honored servant, He will not excuse it in others" (Ibid.).

Adam did a "light thing" also. He reached for a piece of fruit from his wife that God had said, "No, don't eat it!" It was just a small act on Adam's part, but look at all the woe and misery it has brought to our world.

"God dealt so severely with this sin in His most faithful and honored servant [Moses], He will not excuse it in others. The spirit of self-exaltation, the disposition to censure our brethren, is displeasing to God …. The more important one's position, and the greater his influence, the greater is the necessity that he should cultivate patience and humility" (Ibid.).

23

So Close

Ahead lay the land of Edom and the traveling nation knew the Edomites were not only friends, they were relatives, descendants of Esau, the brother of Jacob. They believed in the same God. Part of their land could actually be seen, and it was green. And green meant water, not sand. The Israelites began to sigh and relax, the going would be easier now and the cloud pointed straight ahead.

Moses sent an envoy to Edom's king. He stated their route would lead through his land and asked for permission to cross it. Nothing would be touched. There would be no trouble of any kind. It would be an orderly and peaceful crossing. They would also pay for whatever food and water they needed as they traveled through their country. This was the answer, "Thou shalt not pass by me, lest I come out against thee with the sword" (Num. 20:18).

Moses was amazed and overwhelmed. A second request was sent with the same reply but with this addition: Armed soldiers were posted at all the entrances, sending a clear message that the Children of Israel could not pass through.

Now, what were they to do?

The Lord had ordered a peaceful advance without force. So, once more the Israelites began to complain and murmur. They showed no faith in God's Word and went against His leading. Fear ruled. "... Israel again turned toward the south, and made their way over sterile wastes, that seemed even more dreary after a glimpse of the green spots among the hills and valleys of Edom" (*Patriarchs and Prophets*, p. 424).

If they had "... passed through Edom, as God had purposed, the passage would have proved a blessing, not only to themselves, but to the inhabitants of the land; for it would have given them an opportunity to become acquainted with God's people and His worship and to witness how the God of Jacob prospered those who loved and feared [obeyed] Him" (Ibid.).

Moses and Aaron were both disappointed in the decision not to go into Edom. They had been so close to the Promised Land, so close and now, as the nation turned southward, they found traveling extremely hazardous. Off in the distance they could barely see Mount Hor looming ahead of them. With progress, that mountain arose closer and higher until it seemed to be beside them. It was here that God revealed to Moses that Aaron's life would soon end on that mountain. His words were, "Take Aaron and Eleazar his son, and bring them up unto Mount Hor: and strip Aaron of his garments [his priestly robes], and put them upon Eleazar his son: and Aaron shall be gathered unto his people, and shall die there" (Ibid., p. 425).

This was not easy for Moses. But after the camp settled at the foot of the mountain, the three men began to climb. It was hard going for the two older, white-haired men, the brothers Moses and Aaron. Eleazar had no difficulty as he helped his father and Moses up the long climb. These two aged men had seen much together. They shared many rough trials and dangers. With tact and dignity, and under the guidance of divine power, great natural abilities had been developed in both. The brothers were unselfish, firm, noble and possessed strong affection for each other and all who came under their influence. Aaron had sinned greatly, that's true, but he had also been forgiven much. Now, old and tired, God was still first in his mind. Everything he did and thought was of God. Love to the Lord of heaven and earth motivated his every move.

But now, he and Moses were to be separated by death. "When Aaron died, one of the most illustrious men that ever lived, there were only two of his nearest friends to witness his death and to attend his burial" (Ibid., p. 427). Aaron died in the arms of Moses, his brother. There were tears, many tears, as Moses and Aaron's son Eleazar buried him. "And that lonely grave upon Mount Hor was forever hidden from the sight of Israel [and the world]" (Ibid.).

Many were the thoughts that ran through the mind of Moses as he and Eleazar slowly moved down the mountainside. It had been close to forty years of wandering in desert wastelands. There were triumphs and defeats, many of both, but in spite of Israel's insistent murmuring, God was always there for them. He never left them, not once. This was evident, especially when the nation complained and rebelled. He was especially with them also when they obeyed. The Israelites were a hard people to lead. Most seemed ready and determined to do as they pleased, but when the going got rough, they submitted and made promises to do as God wanted only to later break their promises when things went well again. Fickle one day, obedient the next and unthankful for all the benefits they enjoyed. Manna was complained about, yet God never stopped the supply. They often pointed fingers at God longing for the flesh pots of Egypt, the great foods their fathers and grandfathers told them about. Some wanted to go back. Would this unstable, ever-on-the-move condition ever end? They were a real pain to themselves and others.

These two aged men had seen much together. They shared many rough trials and dangers. With tact and dignity, and under the guidance of divine power, great natural abilities had been developed in both. The brothers were unselfish, firm, noble and possessed strong affection for each other and all who came under their influence.

Moses' thoughts may have gone like this. "I am an old man, and I know I will never see, or even touch the Promised Land, but if that is

God's wish, then so be it. He is my Friend and always has been. My one and only true Friend. I can't, and I won't let Him down. I'm tired, ancient as some say I am, and alone, but He knows that too. God and I must and will go on wherever it takes us." And the cloud pointed forward.

Trouble loomed ahead as they neared Canaanite lands with its king named Arad. And sure enough, there was a fight and they lost. But the cloud had indicated they should go ahead anyway. So, now what? Should they continue as He told them? But the people were united this time, and they begged the Lord for help and guidance. It was given. They fought the Canaanites a second time, and with God beside them, won.

But they were not thankful to Him for this victory. God had heard their pleas and gave them success. But instead of praising Him for it, they became proud and self-confident. Complaints broke out again. Angry voices shouted that there had been no need for all those bitter years of traveling in barren, dry deserts. Those hardships were not necessary. Thousands of unmarked graves lay beneath the sands. "Why?" they cried. Angry chanting voices rebelled again. They shouted they should have invaded the Promised Land years ago and made it their own. Now they had proof they could have done it. "Didn't we just win against Arad and the Canaanites?!" they roared.

So here we go again. Would they ever learn? "And the people spake against God, and against Moses, Wherefore have ye brought us up out of Egypt to die in the wilderness? for there is no bread, neither is there any water; and our soul loatheth this [the MEV versions says worthless] light bread [manna]" (Num. 21:5). Arrogance and pride were the rule of the day.

Naturally, living in the heart of the desert had been hard and unrelenting but, on the other hand, so were they a hard and unrelenting people. Here they were again with the same old complaints from Satan. The bickering never changed. These people didn't seem to be aware of the dangers surrounding them in the desert.

God had protected them from wild beasts, things that crawl, lack of food and water. He gave shade from burning heat, warmth, and light during cold nights. Their feet never felt the blistering sand and clothing never wore out. There was always enough food, water, and shelter. Miracle of all miracles, God saw to all of these things, and they took them without one word of thanks. They acted as if they deserved it.

Then because of their constant whining, self-pity, fault finding and never-ending grumbling they caused God to pull His protection away. They were left on their own. The Lord allowed death to enter the camp. Swarms of poisonous snakes crawled all around them. They stepped on them, found them in tents, on beds, even in their food, and those miserable things bit. No one or place was safe. They died by the thousands and things were growing worse. Terror was on every face as screams of the dying filled their ears. Those horrible things slithered everywhere.

People knew what they had done. Thousands began humbling themselves before God pleading for forgiveness and help. They went to Moses crying, "We have sinned! We have spoken against God and you!" (Num. 21:7). Now, instead of being their worst enemy, Moses was their only hope for asking God to stop the miserable plague of death.

Moses was instructed by God to make a brass serpent and lift it high on a pole for all to see. And if anyone would look at it, they would live. Those who did not, would die. Even then, those who scoffed, died. But all who had been bitten and looked, lived. People were aware that this brass serpent had no power to heal. Only God could do that. Jesus referred to the significance of this hundreds of years later in his conversation with Nicodemus when he said "And as Moses lifted up the serpent in the wilderness, even so must the Son of man be lifted up."

But Moses was asking them to show faith in God by doing what He asked them to do. They were to look and believe. It was a simple act of faith on their part. And when they obeyed and did look, He healed them and removed the trouble.

"Faith is the gift of God, but the power to exercise it is ours .... When we trust God fully, when we rely upon the merits of Jesus as a sin-pardoning Savior, we shall receive all the help that we can desire .... At this very time He is inviting us to come to Him in our helplessness and be saved" (Ibid., p. 431).

24

Giants

With the brass serpent and all the snakes gone, the way north to the Promised Land was open. Here now were a happy people with high hopes for the future. They were in tune with God at last and Moses sighed with relief, but he didn't hold his breath. He knew them and had seen this kind of attitude before. Lessons, serious lessons had been learned, but would they stick? The road ahead was not paved with roses. Ruts and thorns, many thorns, were in the way.

To the east was the land of Moab. They were told not to enter or disturb it, only pass it by. The descendants there were of Lot's family. It was the same when they reached the Ammonite territory. Its people were also descendants of Lot.

Once again, trouble, great trouble, would block their way. The Amorite nation lay directly across their path. Of all the people in that part of the world, these were the most feared. Wild, ruthless, warlike, they welcomed and thirsted for a good fight and they were more than equipped to carry out their threats.

Moses sent peace-feelers to their king. He asked for safe passage through his country. The monarch roared with laughter and called out his troops. He forbade and dared any one of the Israelites to step foot on his land. If they did, it meant war and he was ready (Num. 21:22, 23).

Like jagged streaks of lightning, fear ran through the Hebrews. But Moses had a steady eye and was strong as ever. He kept his patience as he studied the movement of the cloud. It moved forward as he gave orders for all to prepare for war.

The Lord told Moses, "This day will I begin to put the dread of thee and the fear of thee upon the nations that are under the whole heaven, who shall hear report of thee, and shall tremble, and be in anguish because of thee" (Deut. 2:25).

The Lord gave orders to cross the Arnon River. The Lord gave orders to cross the Arnon River. "The Arnon River flows through the present *Wadi el Mojib*, which is some 1,700 ft. deep and 2 mi. broad, cut into the plateau of Moab. Its gorge is a miniature Grand Canyon" (*The SDA Bible Commentary*, vol. 1, p. 895). True to His Word, the Lord went into battle with the Israelites and won the entire country of the Amorites. Their people and armies were completely destroyed.

Now, a new attitude spread over the Hebrews. They saw that when they obeyed God, things went their way. This gave them hope. Finally, and at last, faith plus belief began to take hold and become part of their everyday life. With victory behind them, nothing seemed to hold them back and they went forward with the hope of never living in desert wastes again. God and His Israelite people were coming together at last in one name, action, and spirit.

Ahead, however, lay a challenge that would severely test their newfound faith. It was the kingdom of Bashan. Bashan was known by all nations near and far as the land of giants. If Moab was the terror of the Middle East in those days, then Bashan was the terror of the world. They had towering, walled cities. Their houses, even outside city walls, were built from tremendously large and very black stones. This gave a sinister appearance. Being constructed to resist attack, they were considered unconquerable.

It was a wild country. Its terrain was filled with extremely high cliffs, canyons, caves, deep hollow gullies, and large unnumbered, heavily fortified fortresses where armies could hide. But it was the people who were the greatest threat. There were hundreds of thousands of them living like vast swarms of grasshoppers. They seemed to cover the entire earth. There was no end of them. Worse than this, here was a race of excessive height. They were giants, massive and well known for their powerful strength. And they loved wickedness, fighting and cruelty. Their king, Og, even in his nation of giants, was a violent man, massive in height and size. His strength was more powerful than almost all others, and he was known for his ruthless, pitiless brutality. No one, not even his own people could withstand him. He was fearful to behold and fearless in action.

The Israelites were more than scared, but the cloud and Moses said, "Forward!" And forward it was. The cloud too, with every step they took, seemed to grow larger and taller than ever. And Moses, without hesitation, followed behind it, silent, face set and with a look of "no turning back." Moses, his quiet unfailing faith was a tower of strength for all who saw him. He was their leader and they were proud of it. The Hebrew army followed, trembling and frightened, but determined with their renewed faith, they marched forward and never looked back.

No one knows just how it happened, but it did. That brute of a king and his army, strong as they were, were no match for God and His people. The Israelites won the battle and the entire kingdom as well. Their enemies had been completely destroyed and the earth was a far better and safer place.

Ahead stood the vast armies of the enemy. Thousands upon thousands of fighting men ready, waiting, eager and thirsting for battle. And Og, giant of all giants, towered above his men and waited. But Moses, calm and confident, remembered what God had told him. He said, "Do not fear him, for I will deliver him and all his people and his land, into your hand" (Deut. 3:2, MEV).

No one knows just how it happened, but it did. That brute of a king and his army, strong as they were, were no match for God and His people.

The Israelites won the battle and the entire kingdom as well. Their enemies had been completely destroyed and the earth was a far better and safer place. The heathen worshipers, followers of Satan, were erased before them along with their iniquity and hideous, revolting idolatry.

The Hebrew people had seen so much. They learned bitter lessons from their fathers and grandfathers before them who had not gone into the Promised Land as God pointed the way. Instead, they failed and lived years of wilderness hardships until most rebels had died off. Not so now. The children, the younger generation of those fallen, were now ready to follow anywhere God led. They believed.

But even then it would not be easy, and they knew it. Years of time had given heathen nations liberty to arm themselves and prepare for their advance. Yet even then, and sad as it was, as battles erupted, not a few of the younger set of Israel lost their life.

As is often the case, the second time around is better than the first. With their coming of age, the younger members of the Hebrew race were of a different attitude. As they grew taller and older, they observed and learned from the mistakes of the past. And now, hard as it would be, they were ready to go forward in faith with God. The traveling tabernacle, the holy ark was in their midst, plus God's chosen one, Moses, their leader was still with them.

25

The Donkey Asked Why

Thus far, you have read a good number of pages about Moses and the Hebrew nation. But, for a page or two more, let us take a look at the other side. And what do I mean by that? My answer is the Moabite nation. They believed, or should I say, they used to believe in the same God the Israelites did. Their ancestry was the same. The line began with Abraham; however, they forsook God and withdrew from Him by going deep into the idolatry of other nations. They apostatized.

Even then they were curious because through the years they closely followed the progress of the Israelites and were well aware of everything that happened to them. However, the big question was, what about their God? Who was He?

Now, with the Hebrews practically next door, they were terror-stricken. They trembled with fear wondering what would happen to them. Would they be attacked as were other nations? It was a real possibility. So, what could they do to stop these unstoppable people and their God? They knew they were no match against them if it came to a fight. Defeating them was out of the question. For this God of theirs was on their side. He was leading and protecting them.

Someone reported to Balak the Moabite king that a man named Balaam was one of their God's prophets. That was true except for one thing, he was a prophet gone wrong. He no longer served the Hebrew God, yet he pretended to be just that, God's prophet. So, the king sent for him to put a curse on the Israelites. This might stop an invasion. Money, a bribe, lots of it, fame and great power were offered Balaam if he would come (Num. 22:4–6).

This false prophet was not dumb. He delayed. This gave time for a better deal. And his greedy plan worked. Balaam knew perfectly well he could never put a curse on the Israelites. It would not work anyway, even if he knew how to do it.

God stepped in at this point and told Balaam to go to the king, and as he did so, God would control Balaam's words. Balaam rode his donkey to see the king. The animal stopped three different times on the road and refused to move or take one step farther. Balaam was furious. He beat the poor animal severely. He even told the animal he would kill him with a sword if he had one.

While this was going on, the Lord did something unusual, and He might have smiled as He did so. He gave the donkey a human voice. The animal opened its mouth and asked Balaam "Why are you beating me? What have I done to you?" (Num. 22:28).

Can anyone imagine such a thing? Here was an animal with a human voice and it was speaking to Balaam. And, of all things, this man was silly enough to answer and think nothing of it.

Suddenly, while this was going on, the Lord appeared with a sword in His hand and He was threatening Balaam with it. This was what the donkey had seen the three times he stopped on the road. It had seen the Lord standing on the road ahead, pointing a sword at Balaam.

Balaam, scared to death by now, dropped to the ground and begged for his life. The Lord then stepped aside, allowing him to go on his way. But He reminded Balaam that the words he would speak to the king would not be his own. They would be God's words. That talking animal had actually saved Balaam's life and he didn't even know it.

Later, when Balaam stood on a high cliff with the king and his army overlooking Israel, he opened his mouth and in a loud voice began to speak. But the words tumbling from his lips were blessings, not curses.

The Israelites were unaware of what was going on. This shows that God was not only with the Hebrew nation, He was also protecting them from the evil that surrounded them.

God does the same for His people today. No matter where they are or what problems they face, He is always there—that is, if they want Him there. But, and I use the word but, Balaam was not finished with his plans to destroy the Israelites and gain the wealth and power offered him. Greed and lust still ruled him. Although he was banished by the king of Moab, Balaam returned to him once more with an evil, diabolical plan. He said it would work. This plan delighted the king so much that he, without question, accepted the plan.

Let's switch scenes for a moment and look in on the Israelites while this was going on. God was leading from the cloud and Moses knew nothing of the trouble nearby. Satan and Balaam, who was another Judas, were both hard at work with plans to destroy God's people. And there was no donkey to warn Balaam this time.

Balaam was amazed when he saw the size of the Israelite camp. He was told they were made up of small groups or little bands raising havoc across the countryside. But what he saw from his high position on the mountainside was a vast sea of highly organized thousands. Row upon row of neat, clean tents stretched as far as his eyes could see and sitting to one side was the tabernacle tent. This was God's doing and he knew that nothing on earth could rival God's might and power.

But he had a plan and he felt it would work. He told King Balak that if they could entice the Hebrews into idolatry, to worship false gods, then they would become weak and could be overpowered. If they turned to heathenism, God, the God of heaven would not fight for them. By doing this the Israelites would have turned their backs on the only One who protected and cared for their every move. God would not be their God any longer and they would become helpless on their own.

Sadly, Balaam's thinking was right. The Israelite encampment was on a plain that ran for several miles beside the Jordan River. It was a wide, sheltered valley and tropical in climate. Acacia groves and other trees rich in fruit were plentiful. This was a haven of rest for them with pleasant surroundings. They loved it and began to relax on it. Moses was totally engrossed in plans for the occupation of Canaan and the people were left to themselves to think about their future. They had time on their hands which, in truth, became a deadly trap.

Surrounding them in this beautiful place were heathen neighbors. And Balaam was quietly doing his deceptive work among them. Under his direction, Midianite women began appearing among the Hebrews (Num. 25:1–5). It was done slyly at first and no one took much notice, even Moses. The aim, the job of these women was to slowly introduce their rites and customs among the Hebrews. This would lead to idolatry. Soon after their arrival, idols and shrines were in permanent places and the Israelites slowly became accustomed to seeing them. These women did this under seemingly innocent but false friendship. Their quiet, gentle, and convincing ways along with their make-believe show of pleasant relationship was easily accepted without question. They were successful and gained Israelite trust.

> At Balaam's suggestion, a grand festival in honor of their gods was appointed by the king of Moab [Balak], and it was secretly arranged that Balaam should induce [urge] the Israelites to attend. He was regarded by them as a prophet of God, and hence had little difficulty in accomplishing his purpose. Great numbers of the people joined him in witnessing the festivities. They ventured upon the forbidden ground, and were entangled in the snare of Satan. (*Patriarchs and Prophets*, p. 454)

Scenes much too graphic for description followed. Suggestive dancing, wild, loud music, drunkenness, and open sexual passions took over. It climaxed with the disgrace of many of God's people bowing down and worshiping idols. When the news of this massive apostasy reached Moses, with the full extent of its activities explained to him, he fell into a violent rage. This festival had not only been eagerly welcomed and accepted by many Israelites, but great numbers of its leaders embraced it as well.

Pagan shrines had been slyly erected and idol worship was becoming widespread throughout the entire camp.

Somehow Moses had not seen it. No one told him. The furious, uncontrolled reaction by Moses was immediately followed by a deadly epidemic from God. People were struck instantly without warning. And thousands upon thousands died. Those not affected raced to the tabernacle, begging God to forgive them. They knew this punishment for wrongdoing was just. They deserved it. With deep humility and tears running down their faces, they confessed their sins and sincerely meant every word they uttered, and these were the people who a short time before were ready to enter the Promised Land.

Moses pled with God to stop the plague before the entire nation was destroyed. As a result, God withdrew His plague but only after leaders of the apostasy had been executed. But the story does not end yet. It continues. The Midianite nation was the cause of this apostasy. Thus, by divine order the Israelites were to prepare for battle against them. Each tribe was to provide 1,000 soldiers to do the fighting.

As a result, five kings of Midian were destroyed along with their armies. And as a special point of interest, Balaam, the renegade, traitor prophet was also killed with them. Israel "… brought the judgments of God upon the nation, and though the same sins may not now be punished [today] as speedily, they will as surely meet retribution" (Ibid., p. 461).

When God gave the order to destroy the Midianite people, He added a personal note to Moses. We read it in Numbers 31:2, "… afterward shalt thou be gathered unto thy people."

Moses was going to die. This devastated Moses and it haunted him for many, many days. The greatest desire of his heart, besides loving and doing God's will, was to lead God's people into the land He promised. Now after years and years of hardship and pain, it would not happen. It was his fault, and he knew it.

Not long after this he heard the call, "It's time."

26

It Is Time

It was time and Moses knew it. Death was calling. But he, like most humans, did not want this to happen. He had no fear of death, no, that was not the case. He pled with God, "Not now Lord, not yet." He earnestly called, "Please, not now." What Moses wanted most was to see, feel, and walk in the land of promise with His, God's people.

It had been so many years in coming and now that it was within reach, he longed to have the joy of feeling and being on its soil—just once. That's all he asked. Gods answer to his request was, "… [S]peak no more unto me on this matter" (Deut. 3:26).

God's original plan was for the rescued slaves from Egypt to immediately inherit the Promised Land. They were to become His people, a nation of priests, to inform the rest of the world about Him. But that did not happen. His plan never changed; however, it was delayed. This was because of the Israelites themselves. The people were not ready to represent Him as a holy nation and it took forty years and more of wandering in the deserts of Africa until they were ready.

So, what was the reaction of Moses to God's answer? After all they were on a first name basis beside being close friends. Best friends don't talk to each other that way. Moses understood and accepted it without murmur or complaint. Both he and God knew the reason why he was not allowed to enter the Promised Land. He and Aaron had deliberately overstepped their position at the rock of Horeb and the question about authority. By taking credit to themselves for something God had done in providing water from the rock, a penalty had to follow. Theirs was not the right example for the nation who watched. And they were watching.

It was especially wrong coming from the leaders of that traveling nation. They had taken over God's power and claimed it as their own. Although they had been forgiven, it could not go unnoticed. There had to be punishment for what they did. If not, it would have given a false example to the Israelites and others that God was not in control in that or any other situation. This had directly pointed to the ego of the human heart. In other words, it would be an echo of what Lucifer once said in heaven when he stated that, "I will be like the Most High!" (Isa. 14:14).

Moses was a man ancient in age, hair as white as snow, yet he stood erect, straight, and tall. He was as a young man in the best of health. His eyesight was perfect, and yet he was almost 120 years old. Deeply in love with God, he pled with every fiber in his body for what lay heavy on his heart. He was not begging for his life to be prolonged; he knew better. God had already settled that. And it had nothing to do with himself except for the influence and leadership of something he was so intimately and emotionally attached to. It was for the future of God's chosen people, the Hebrew nation. They were his family, his and God's joy, the people who were to shout to the world about God, explaining His true nature in all the universe. They were the chosen race of priests, showing and living, not for themselves only, but for the One who was everything, their all in all.

Moses was in love with each and every person of the Hebrew nation. They were like children to him. What would happen to them now?

Who would be there to guide them? He, as their leader and spokesman for God, was going to leave them without anyone to tell them what God wanted them to do, say and be. He knew and accepted the fact that he was about to lose his life, but the one thing, the one and only thought so heavily on his heart and mind was for God's chosen people, the Israelite nation. "Who, Lord, who?" was his cry. "Oh, God," he wept, "You are the only true God; who is there to lead them now? Don't abandon them to themselves alone. They are wandering in dangerous places. They are helpless. Please, God, choose someone to take my place. But who? Who is there? Your children need You more now than at any other time."

Moses continued, and I must add that the words I have just written and will write are my own. Thus, I have taken the liberty of putting them into his mouth as I feel he would have said and felt them. This is the real Moses.

I feel Moses must have broken into tears at this point that ran like streams of water across his face, down his clothing to splash on the ground in a pool of water. And God did answer his pleading, "Take thee Joshua the son of Nun, a man in whom is the spirit, and lay thine hand upon him; and set him before Eleazar the priest, and before all the congregation; and give him a charge in their sight" (Num. 27:18, 19).

Joshua was a fighting man and known as a fearless warrior. He was a force to be reckoned with. He was powerful, strong, and muscular, but best and most of all he was completely firm in his faith to God. Joshua had been the right-hand man of Moses for years and knew the ways of God. Unwavering in his loyalty, he stood ready to do whatever God asked of him.

Evidence for his complete loyalty to God is found in chapters 24 and 32 of Exodus. Those chapters state that Joshua and Moses had been asked to climb Mount Sinai. Recall how they were gone for forty days on that same mountain? Well we find them doing it again, only this time it would not be for forty days. Slowly and quietly they began their long, unhurried climb. There was not much conversation.

Moses struggled with every step across the face of the mountain. And the higher and farther they climbed, the smaller they appeared from below. People were watching. Then they were lost from sight. Wind moaned in their ears. It was windy near the top, it tossed the white hair of Moses behind him then whipped it about his face. He rested often. Finally, they stopped below the summit. They faced each other. Moses knew his work was over. They must have talked, but there is no record of what they said.

The adopted son of Pharaoh's daughter, ruler of Israel was about to close his eyes, joining those who had hoped to dwell in a land flowing with milk and honey but never made it. Joshua knew the end was near for the friend he loved. They held each other tightly. Joshua didn't want to let go. He hung on with his strong arms.

Moses slowly and tenderly released him whispering, "God is calling."

With misty eyes Joshua watched as Moses carefully removed his cloak, a symbol of authority, folded it and gently placed it in the hands of Joshua. Next his outstretched hand placed it in those same hands of his beloved Joshua. They didn't speak; they couldn't. Moses turned for a last look down and across that vast, seemingly endless Hebrew nation. This view lasted only for a moment. God was calling again.

"I'm coming," he whispered, "I'm coming."

With Joshua watching he began his last climb. After a few steps he stopped, turned, and looking at Joshua still holding the cloak and staff said, "Listen to God and lead His people wisely." He hesitated then added, "And be gentle."

Joshua said nothing as he watched Moses make his final steps up the mountain. Rounding a small rise and descending its other side, Moses vanished from sight. He was gone.

Joshua sat with face in hands and tears flowed. The staff and cloak were beside him. Reaching for something to dry his eyes, his hand touched the cloak of Moses. Straightening himself he stood, reached for the cloak and staff, and began a slow descent. He stopped only once to look back to the last place he saw this great man, his friend.

The people below saw him coming with that cloak and staff. They knew and began to wail, the sound reaching high on the mountainside. Their beloved Moses was gone.

God with Joshua was their leader now.

Afterword

I planned to end the story of Moses, the desert prince, with chapter 26, but I found there is more to tell. Or should I just say, the best is yet to come.

When Moses finally reached the top of that mountain, he was tired, so he sat down to rest and wait for what was to come next. He knew his life was about to end. No longer had he got seated and leaned back on the rock behind him when a powerful explosion of light exploded all around him. It just about blinded his eyes.

When his eyes could focus again, he felt he could see forever even far beyond distant horizons. (It was almost like a giant TV screen that ran for miles.) He was looking across the land God had promised and it stretched sharp and clear mile after mile, hundreds of them. Gasping in unbelief by what he saw stretching to far distant horizons in every direction, lay the land God promised. And it was clear and sharp.

Ellen White describes the scene. "Far away to the west lay the blue waters of the Great Sea; in the north, Mount Hermon stood out against the sky; to the east was the tableland of Moab, and beyond lay Bashan, the scene of Israel's triumph; and away to the south stretched the desert of their long wanderings" (*Patriarchs and Prophets*, p. 471).

> He seemed to be looking upon a second Eden. There were mountains clothed with cedars of Lebanon, hills gray with olives and fragrant with the odor of the vine, wide green plains bright with flowers and rich in fruitfulness, here the palm trees of the tropics, there waving fields of wheat and barley, sunny valleys

musical with the ripple of brooks and the song of birds, goodly cities and fair gardens, lakes rich in "the abundance of the seas," grazing flocks upon the hillsides, and even amid the rocks the wild bee's hoarded treasures. (Ibid., p. 472)

Moses was looking at time that had not yet happened, the future. As he stared in disbelief, he saw Joshua leading the Israelites as they stepped on their new land. Ahead lay dangers, trials, hardships, happiness, failures, wars, triumphs, and defeats, but for now there were only shouts of joy, not the screams of battle.

Moses was also given another vision. In this he was shown the future of the Israelites, for as they were comfortably settled in the Promised Land, apostasy would raise its ugly head again.

He was also shown the first advent of Christ, Gethsemane, the crucifixion, the resurrection, and Jesus' return in triumph to heaven. "And it was there revealed to him that he himself would be one who should attend the Saviour, and open to Him the everlasting gates [of Heaven]" (Ibid., p. 476).

His vision of the future continued on down through the centuries even to the end of earth's final days. He saw the second coming, and views of the new earth. "… [T]he vision faded, and his eyes rested upon the land of Canaan as it spread out in the distance. Then, like a tired warrior, he lay down to rest. So Moses the servant of the Lord died there in the land of Moab, according to the word of the Lord. And He [God] buried him in a valley in the land of Moab, over against Beth-peor: but no man knoweth of his sepulcher [grave]" (Ibid., p. 477). Deuteronomy 34:6 states that God buried Moses. Other versions read the same.

But there is a statement by Ellen White that reads, "But angels of God buried the body of His [God's] faithful servant and watched over the lonely grave" (Ibid., p. 478). I see no conflict with that. How many times has someone who lost a loved one been asked, "Where did you bury him/her?" Here is my thinking. The one being asked didn't do the work, someone in the business of doing the job did it for them. I will say no more.

Ellen White continues with, "Had not the life of Moses been marred with that one sin, in failing to give God the glory [credit] of bringing water from the rock at Kadesh, he would have entered the Promised Land, and would have been translated to heaven without seeing death" (Ibid., p. 478).

The passage continues, "But he was not long to remain in the tomb. Christ Himself, with the angels who had buried Moses, came down from heaven to call forth the sleeping saint .... For the first time Christ was about to give life to the dead" (Ibid.).

You have just finished reading a love story and every word of it is true. It ends well, not as the Hollywood people end theirs, but with something all of us hope for, the best of all, eternal life.

A floating basket with a baby inside and the Creator of the universe came together as one. It was a rough and hard road for both, but they did it together. The road is much easier now for they are together in heaven.

Large planets, massive beyond belief, that spin in controlled order as they orbit in magnificent splendor through light years of God's creation all speak of the greatness of God and His condescension to work through one small human. It is not only breathtaking, but unbelievable as well. But this is their story and it has no ending. It is forever.

The strange part is the human in this story. Moses died. But he did not long remain in the grave. He was resurrected. He is thousands of years old and still going. Proof for this fact comes from the Bible itself. Matthew chapter 17, MEV, tells this story.

Jesus took three of His disciples (disciple: one who learns and spreads another's teachings) Peter, James and John to a high mountain and was transfigured (changed in form or appearance) in front of them. Verse 2 reads, "His face shone as the sun, and His garments became white as the light." Verse 3 continues, "Suddenly Moses and Elijah appeared to them, talking with Him."

There you have it (for those who believe in the Bible)! No other proof is needed. Moses is alive.

Love, true and honest, between two individuals is something that never can be fully understood or explained. For example, when Adam and

Eve turned their back on God and walked away, He could have destroyed them on the spot. He didn't do that. There are many reasons why. One reason is that others were watching and would have thought, *I better watch it, or he will do the same to me.* God doesn't function that way. He loved Adam and Eve so much that He formed a plan that took the life of His only Son to save them from a forever death. That is love. Sorry to say, there are only a very few who believe and live this way.

David and Jonathan knew and lived this, and sex had no part in their love for each other. It was pure and honest. Jesus and John also understood it. Even Ellen White referred to it by calling it "mysterious links" that tie two beings together, one answering the needs and wants and desires of each other (sex excluded) (*Adventist Home*, p. 455). The government of God is based on this.

When Moses was raised back to life it was not in the form he left behind. That was still in the grave. He was a new, glorious, glowing creature with a robe of dazzling light and filled with great intellect and powerful energy, but most of all he was with the One he truly loved the most—GOD!

Bibliography

Josephus, Titus Flavius. *The Works of Flavius Josephus, Book I.* New York: Whitsom, Hurst, & Co. Publishers.

Wells, Albert. *Genealogical Chronology of the World Before Christ.* Edited by K.A. McMurdo. London: W.H. Allen, 1889.

White, Ellen G. *Christ's Object Lessons.* Review and Herald Publishing Association, 1900.

———. *Education.* Mountain View, CA: Pacific Press Publishing Association, 1903.

———. "Journeyings of the Israelites." *The Signs of the Times*, April 8, 1880.

———. *Patriarchs and Prophets.* Mountain View, CA: Pacific Press Publishing Association, 1890.

———. *The Desire of Ages.* Mountain View, CA: Pacific Press Publishing Association, 1898.

———. *The Great Controversy.* Mountain View, CA: Pacific Press Publishing Association, 1911.

———. *The SDA Bible Commentary.* Vol. 1. Washington, DC: Review and Herald Publishing Association, 1953.

———. *The SDA Bible Commentary.* Vol. 5. Washington, DC: Review and Herald Publishing Association, 1956.

———. *The SDA Bible Commentary.* Vol. 7. Washington, DC: Review and Herald Publishing Association, 1957.

TEACH Services, Inc.
P U B L I S H I N G
www.TEACHServices.com • (800) 367-1844

We invite you to view the complete
selection of titles we publish at:
www.TEACHServices.com

We encourage you to write us
with your thoughts about this,
or any other book we publish at:
info@TEACHServices.com

TEACH Services' titles may be purchased in
bulk quantities for educational, fund-raising,
business, or promotional use.
bulksales@TEACHServices.com

Finally, if you are interested in seeing
your own book in print, please contact us at:
publishing@TEACHServices.com

We are happy to review your manuscript at no charge.

www.ingramcontent.com/pod-product-compliance
Lightning Source LLC
Chambersburg PA
CBHW031322160426
43196CB00007B/632